Shuttleworth

The aircraft collection

Shuttleworth

The aircraft collection

Photography
John M. Dibbs

Text
Martin W. Bowman

Airlife
England

British Library Cataloguing-in-Publication Data

A catalogue record for this book is available from the British Library

ISBN 1 84037 072 6

Design concept by John Dibbs

Page layout and graphics by Robert Wilcockson

Printed in Hong Kong

Airlife Publishing Ltd

101 Longden Road, Shrewsbury, SY3 9EB, England

E-mail: airlife@airlifebooks.com

Website: www.airlifebooks.com

Cover: Shuttleworth's Spitfire V, Lysander III and Gladiator slip through a summer evening
sky, flown by Dave Mackay, 'Dodge' Bailey and John Allison respectively.

For Andy Patsalides - who has known me from my 'dustings' days to sitting
next to the 'Rocket'. He was the first to believe in me and gave me my break.
Thanks for everything.

Acknowledgements

As you can imagine to keep such a fantastic and unique collection of aircraft
together let alone airborne, takes the skill and dedication of a special kind of
people. Add to the pressures of 'normal' operations (if the word 'normal' can
be applied to Old Wardens activities!) the need to fly photographic sorties, and
you really start to test the system. This book therefore is a testament to the
special band of people that make Shuttleworth a reality for the rest of us. I
wish to extend my thanks and appreciation to Andy Sephton and all the pilots
who are able enough, lucky enough and privileged to fly these machines, and
who so patiently assisted me in capturing the images that fill the book.
Tony Haig-Thomas was a great support, as was Chris Morris and his engineers
and volunteers, who against the odds keep our aviation heritage alive and in the
air. Karen and the behind the scenes support kept things ticking over nicely
and were always happy to help. Thanks also to Betty whose shop sales
generate some of the essential funds to keep these aircraft flying.
Thanks to you all.

I also owe thanks to Dennis and Trish Neville, John Romain, Chris Parker and
Brian Skillicorn for wheeling me around the skies so safely and skilfully in the
various cameraships. I also hope Desmond Penrose has thawed out now after
the epic 'Arrow Active' sortie! Special thanks to
Andy Sephton for organising the whole shooting programme.

Photographic support was on hand from John Dickens and Pentax (UK),
Peter Bowerman at CCS (Holdalls) and Graham Armitage at Sigma (UK).

I would also like to thank Ian Frimston, David Macready and
Martin Bowman for their contributions and as ever the support and
hard work on production of Pam Dibbs, Rachel Wisby and Faye Mills.
I'm also grateful to 'Toad' and Rob Wilcockson.

John M. Dibbs
March 2000

Martin Bowman would particularly like to thank Ken Hyde, Chris Morris,
Andy Sephton, Tony Podmore and Karen Wilsher of the Shuttleworth Trust,
and also Mike Gayfer.

1912 Blackburn. ▶

Contents

◀ Arrow Active.

History

tepping through the gates of the Shuttleworth Collection is like crossing the boundaries of history. Time flies at this tranquil airfield of Old Warden in pastoral Bedfordshire. Cricket is still played on the village green nearby, just as it has been for hundreds of years. At Cardington, a short biplane ride away, the gigantic airship sheds built to house the R101 rise up on the grass fields like monstrous dark hills on the horizon. Picnickers enjoy their tea and sandwiches as Moths, Swallows and Sopwiths motor overhead on balmy summer evenings when Old Warden hosts a Sunset Flying Day. There are also military pageants, Flying Proms, a Steam Fayre and a Vintage Transport Day. Horseless carriages and historic vehicles (some dating back to the 1890s), with their drivers and passengers in period costume, often make a welcome appearance alongside the wonderful biplanes and monoplanes.

Richard Ormonde Shuttleworth, in whose memory the Shuttleworth Remembrance Trust is named, was born at Old Warden Park, an imposing Jacobian-style mansion in Bedfordshire, on 16 July 1909, nine days before Louis Blériot's flight across the English Channel. His mother Dorothy was the twenty-three-year old daughter of Old Warden's vicar Bob Lang, one-time cricketer and fastest bowler in England. She had caught the eye of the sixty-three-year-old squire Frank Shuttleworth, who had inherited half the fortune created by his father Joseph. With Nathaniel Clayton, Joseph Shuttleworth had produced the first portable steam-powered agricultural machinery during the 1840s. Frank Shuttleworth died in January 1913, leaving Richard to be brought up by his mother. In 1916 the Clayton & Shuttleworth company became involved with aircraft production. At the Stamp End works in Lincoln, the company built 46 Sopwith Triplanes and 575 Sopwith Camels, as well as some of the giant Handley Page 0/400 bombers.

By the early 1920s, Richard had, with special tuition, managed to pass the entrance exam for Eton College. However, he often failed to attend lessons and sports, or arrived late, covered in oil and grime from the workshops. His lack of academic ability led to his being asked to leave after two years. Nevertheless, the College's then radical School of Mechanics and the elderly third form tutor J.H.M. 'Bunny' Hare were probably responsible for fanning the flames of a burning obsession with all things mechanical that lasted for the rest of Richard's life.

It was decided that Richard should enter the Army like his father before him, but further coaching was necessary to pass the Sandhurst entry exams. Thus, Richard was enrolled at Lathbury Park 'Crammer' not far from Old Warden Park. His mechanical interests continued somewhat illegally with a motorcycle hidden in a barn at Sherrington nearby. In 1927, on his eighteenth birthday, Richard joined the 16/5th Lancers. He also found time to acquire a whole string of vintage automobiles that today forms part of the Shuttleworth Collection. Many of them, with Richard at the wheel, took part in several London–Brighton vintage car runs. By 1930, of ten vehicles owned, five had been entered in the annual outing.

In 1927, George Stead, a New Zealander serving in the RAF, gave Richard his first flight in a Moth biplane. The young Shuttleworth was hooked! In January 1931 he took his first flying lessons at the Scottish Flying Club at Moorpark Aerodrome, Renfrewshire. He received official instruction from

George Lowdell at Brooklands, as well as some unofficial tuition from Stead and Billy Blake in a Moth and a Robinson Redwing. In 1931 the ever adventurous Richard took up motor racing too, entering his first race on 14 March under the pseudonym R. Ormonde to avoid his mother's disapproval. (In 1931 the Warden Engineering Co. was established at Old Warden to prepare Richard's racing cars.) Over the next five years, Richard entered some sixty motor racing events. In characteristic manner, he drove foot hard on the boards.

In 1932 Richard inherited his father's and Uncle Alfred's fortunes, which combined, exceeded £2 million (£50 million in today's values). On 14 February he made his first solo flight from Brooklands in DH60 Cirrus Moth G-EBWD, his first aeroplane, which he bought from Brooklands School of Flying for £300 on 21 January. His second purchase was Comper Swift G-ABWE. He was so pleased with the diminutive machine that he promptly became a director of Nick Comper's company. Early in 1933 Richard and George Stead decided to fly G-ABWE to India to take part in the Viceroy's Trophy Race, the Indian equivalent of the King's Cup Air Race. However, two days before departure G-ABWE was damaged in an accident so the flight was undertaken in the Swifts G-ABCY and G-ABPY. The two pilots covered six thousand miles in sixty flying hours spread over twelve days. It was quite an achievement for a pilot of Richard's limited experience.

Early in 1935 Richard formed Warden Aviation at Heston Aerodrome – partly to satisfy a need to commute from Old Warden to Brooklands and partly for charter work. His fleet consisted of three Comper Swifts, three Desoutters and DH84 Dragon G-ACGG, which had been operated by the King's Flight. Although happy to lavish money on his cars and aeroplanes, Richard disliked paying duty to HM Customs and Excise for spares for his Bugattis. More than once he illegally imported spares by air, making unauthorised landings at Brooklands to unload them before travelling on to make 'land-fall' at Heston with 'Nothing to Declare'. Nevertheless, even Richard was rumbled by the Excise Man and prosecuted. Richard advertised from the air at night using the

Dragon carrying neon signs. He formed Aerial Advertising Ltd, but the Government imposed stringent regulations and the operation folded. His hire and charter business suffered too and in November 1935 Richard moved the business to Old Warden to specialise in C of As (Certificates of Airworthiness) and repairs.

In 1935 Richard met Albert Grimmer, a renowned aviator and aircraft repairer, at his local flying club. In 1912–13 Grimmer had repaired and flown a Deperdussin and a Blériot monoplane in the Bedford area but these had been damaged in accidents and had been laid up for twenty years. Richard set about restoring the Blériot with the help of Squadron Leader L.A. 'Jacko' Jackson (Curator and Manager of the Collection 1946–66), who was formerly connected with the Southern Counties Aviation Co. and Sky Trips Ltd, two pleasure flight companies of the early 1920s. He had also previously worked for Blackburn. By mid-1936, the Blériot had been restored to flying condition and had made several long 'hops' between Biggleswade and Slough. The engine's inability to give full power made the aircraft tail heavy so Richard fitted a new propeller and made some adjustments to the valves and carburettor. The troublesome engine was replaced with an original and new Anzani engine that had never been run. In May 1937 Richard demonstrated the Blériot in public for the first time when he 'gatecrashed' the Royal Aeronautical Society Garden Party at Fairey's Great West Aerodrome. Richard was preceded by C.S. 'Chris' Staniland in the prototype Fairey Battle.

Richard Ormonde Shuttleworth RAFVR at the outbreak of war in 1939. ▲

Meanwhile, other aeroplanes arrived at Old Warden. Group Captain (later Air Commodore) Allen Wheeler, one of the sporting pilots of the early days of club flying, who had once owned an SE5a, delivered an antiquated Blackburn Velos. However, after a few flights, it was dismantled for aviation grade wood. A Vickers Virginia bomber bought by Richard was also scrapped and its wood and fittings saved, but Sopwith Dove G-EBKY, a two-seat variant of the legendary Sopwith Pup, survived and is still flying today. G.A. Chamberlain, the owner, had operated the Dove without benefit of a Pilot's Licence or a C of A so Richard swapped it for an ex-barnstormer Avro 504K. In Richard's opinion the only progress aviation had made in twenty-one years was in aeroplanes having a 'higher landing speed'. He restored the Dove to a Pup 'to show how little constructors had progressed', and it flew on 26 February 1938 with Allen Wheeler at the controls.

Richard's budding career as a champion racing driver ended prematurely in January 1936 when he was badly injured during the second South African Grand Prix. He arrived too late to familiarise himself fully with the circuit and a lack of practice meant his Alfa was not prepared adequately. During the race Richard returned to the pits complaining of the car's poor handling but was persuaded to continue for the benefit of the 90,000 crowd. He lost control at about 150 mph and had to jump for his life. He landed on a boulder and suffered severe head injuries, also splitting his leg open to the bone. Richard lay unconscious for nineteen days. Mrs Shuttleworth arrived shortly after he regained consciousness.

Richard contented himself with restoration and a succession of aeroplanes arrived at Old Warden. By 1938 the Blériot and Deperdussin monoplanes were back in flying condition. In 1938 Richard bought a 1912 Blackburn monoplane which had been discovered under a hayrick near Bawtry. The Blackburn was not fully restored until 1949 when Allen Wheeler flew it for the first time. The last two machines to arrive were an Avro 504K and a Hanriot HD1 Scout. In 1937, while on holiday in Belgium, Richard spotted the little Hanriot biplane displayed outside a cinema where the First World War film *Wings* was being shown. He purchased the Scout for £15. The Avro was used to give pleasure rides at five shillings a flight between Luton and Dunstable. Once, when Richard and 'Jacko' tried to take off to return to Old Warden, it failed to get airborne, probably because of an incorrect mixture setting, and it finished upside down in a field.

The Hanriot suffered a similar fate. While at Brooklands it suffered a punctured tyre. Richard and a mechanic replaced the wheel but forgot to insert the split pin that secured it to the axle and while Richard was in mid-flight the Hanriot and wheel parted company! A telephone call was made to Old Warden where a garden party was in progress, so Richard could be warned of his plight. On arrival Richard misinterpreted the desperate, waving arms of his mother's guests to be a request for a display of 'wheeling' or aerobatics. He duly obliged. Unfortunately, the axle dug in on landing and the Hanriot 'promptly rolled into a ball'. The Avro today forms part of the Shuttleworth Collection, and the Hanriot, after a long restoration in the USA by Marvin Hand, is on display at the RAF Museum.

During the Munich Crisis Richard twice attempted to join the RAFVR, but he was rejected because of a slight hearing disability he had received in the crash in South Africa. Typically, at the third medical Richard bribed the orderly 10s not to cover part of his good ear during the hearing test and passed, despite the CMO's (Chief Medical Officer) protestations later that he had twice failed! Richard's considerable experience as a pilot won the CMO over and he was accepted into the RAFVR. Late in November 1939 Richard was called up at forty-eight hours notice and posted to the Central Flying School at Upavon. Bad weather restricted flying so Richard continued with plans to convert some of his vehicles into mobile workshops. Old Warden, meanwhile, was occupied by Shragers in the war years and about 400 reconditioned Percival Proctors and numerous Harvards were tested on the 600 yard square airfield and flown away.

In January 1940 Richard was posted to No. 10 FTS (Flying Training

Supermarine Spitfire Vc. ▶

School) at Tern Hill, Shropshire. In July he was posted to No. 12 OTU (Operational Training Unit) at RAF Benson, which was equipped with war-weary Ansons, Blenheims and Fairey Battles, some of which had been involved in the Battle of France. Not surprisingly therefore, the accident rate was high and many inexperienced pilots burned to death in crashes. On home leave Richard confided to his mother, 'If they continue making us fly these 'planes, in six weeks we'll all be dead.'

Unfortunately, the premonition came true. At 00.15 hours on 2 August 1940, Richard Shuttleworth died in Battle L4971. Had he lived, his considerable mechanical expertise would have seen him transferred to the Engineering Branch, working as a 'prang-basher' investigating flying accidents. On his death Richard's estate passed to his grief-stricken mother. She created the Richard Ormonde Shuttleworth Remembrance Trust on 26 April 1944 to provide a centre for agricultural purposes and for the 'promotion of education and training in the science, practice and history of aviation and automotive transport'.

The five historic machines first acquired by Richard Shuttleworth, together with Moth G-EBWD, form the core of the Collection of thirty-five or so airworthy machines, which span the first fifty years of the twentieth century. The Collection's vehicles and aeroplanes were not open to public view until 1963, although the machines appeared at airshows, rallies and at Royal Aeronautical Society Garden Parties. They have also appeared in films like *Reach for the Sky*, while the Blackburn monoplane and Deperdussin were used in *Those Magnificent Men in their Flying Machines* in 1965. The Blackburn almost came to grief when the German entrant in the movie ran out of control on the ground after losing its tail! The Bristol Boxkite and Avro Triplane replicas built for the film were later acquired for the Collection.

The Shuttleworth Veteran Aeroplane Society is a registered charity and performs restoration projects such as those on Desoutter G-AAPZ and the Blake Bluetit. The Bluetit was creared from a Simmonds Spartan and Avro 504

by the Blake Brothers during their annual leave from West Africa in 1930, and cost just £26 to build. It was never registered, so a period registration is unlikely to be available if a permit to fly is granted following its restoration.

It was at Old Warden that the de Havilland DH88 Comet Racer *Grosvenor House* rebuild project started, but when it proved too much for the Collection's own resources, help came from the British aviation industry and beyond. The gleaming red and white racer won the Sir MacPherson Robertson Melbourne Centenary Air Race which started at Mildenhall on 20 October 1934. Pilots Tom Campbell-Black and C.W.A. Scott completed the 11,300 miles to the Flemington Racecourse in Melbourne and won both the speed and handicap race. Fully restored to airworthy condition, *Grosvenor House* returned to Mildenhall for the US Air Fete in May 1987 – fifty-three years after leaving the airfield for the memorable flight to Australia.

In 1991 the Northern Aeroplane Workshop completed Sopwith Triplane *Dixie II*, described by the late Sir Thomas Sopwith as a 'late production machine' as opposed to a replica! Sea Hurricane Z7015 was restored jointly with the Imperial War Museum at Duxford. The Hurricane and its Merlin III engine are the earliest airworthy examples anywhere.

Richard Shuttleworth is buried in the family grave at St Leonard's Church, overlooking his home and airfield, which still retains the aura of a small 'thirties aerodrome'. On the first Sunday of each summer month the sound of aero engines can be heard when the oldest and slowest aircraft approach within 40 metres of the crowd, while those that do not exceed 110 knots approach no closer than 65 metres. Engine starts using the time honoured handswing or, for the larger engines, with the Huck's Starter (based on a Model T Ford), keep spectators enthralled.

Old Warden on a summer's day is England at its best. Here there is honey still for tea. May the Collection continue to inspire other organisations to preserve and operate airworthy vintage and veteran aircraft in free skies throughout the world.

The Collection

1909 Blériot Type XI

rench Collection. Although not credited with the first officially observed powered flight in Europe – an honour which went to fellow Frenchman Alberto Santos-Dumont on 23 October 1906 – Louis Blériot is forever remembered as the first man to fly an aeroplane across the English Channel, on 25 July 1909. Late in 1908 the *Daily Mail* offered £1,000 to the first pilot to make a flight between England and France. Frenchman Hubert Latham failed his attempt in a monoplane on 19 July 1909 when his Antoinette IV crashed into the sea only a few miles from Calais. Latham was rescued with nothing more than hurt pride, but before he could try again in another Antoinette, Louis Blériot was already making preparations at Les Baraques (Calais) nearby to fly his Blériot Type XI across the Straits of Dover.

This tractor-monoplane (propeller in front), for which Raymond Saulnier is said to have been partly responsible for the design, was powered by a 25 hp Anzani three-cylinder air-cooled semi-radial (fan-type) engine, driving a two-blade propeller made of walnut. The Blériot Type XI's cockpit largely consisted of an inverted cup-shaped fitting called the *cloche*, patented by Blériot in 1908. To this were attached four cables, two of which caused the outer positions of the wing to warp or twist, making the aeroplane bank from side to side. The other two cables operated the elevator at the tail, causing the machine to rise or descend. A vertical rudder at the tail was operated by a foot bar. Despite the fragile nature of the aeroplane, and an engine that was prone to overheating,

Blériot successfully proved the reliability of the machine when he flew the twenty-five miles from Etampes to Orléans on 13 July in preparation for the Channel attempt.

Blériot took off at 4.35 am on Sunday 25 July and just over half an hour later, safely landed in a field in front of Dover Castle. Blériot had flown at a speed of about 40 mph at a height between 150 ft and 300 ft, and had covered a distance of 31 miles. At 9 am the following morning the Blériot monoplane was proudly on display at Selfridge's department store in Oxford Street, London.

The Blériot Type XI (No. 14) which was acquired by Richard Shuttleworth in 1938 is very similar to the one used for the Channel crossing. Powered by a 25 hp Anzani three-cylinder fan from a 1910 Blériot, this aircraft is probably the only example of a genuine Type XI still flying. Other airworthy Blériots are replicas with modern engines. No. 14 is almost certainly one of the original machines from the Blériot School, which opened at Hendon on 1 October 1910. It crashed in 1912 and was acquired by Albert Grimmer, proprietor of the Flitt Motor Co. at Ampthill, Bedfordshire. He rebuilt it and then, using a local polo ground near Bedford, taught himself to fly it. In 1935 the Blériot was removed from a loft over the Flitt Motor Co. premises and Richard Shuttleworth acquired this as his first 'historic' aircraft. The staff at Old Warden completely restored it and the Blériot was flown by Richard Shuttleworth at the RAF Display in 1936. With due reverence to its age and rarity, straight hops only are now permitted, and even then when conditions are perfect.

▲ Rear view of the Blériot Type XI.

Blériot Type XI. ▶

1910 Deperdussin

ntente cordiale. The French Deperdussin single-seat monoplane first caught the public eye at the Paris Aero Salon of October 1910. The show proved the start of a short but glorious career for the Deperdussin and a succession of racing versions became famous for their participation in the 1920s Schneider Trophy contests. The school or 'Popular' Type was exhibited at the Paris Aero Salon in December 1911, together with more powerful two- and three-seat military versions. The British Deperdussin Aviation Company was managed by S.F.W. Kooloven, and Deperdussin aeroplanes were exhibited at the 1913 Olympia Aero Show.

The Collection's 1910 'Popular' version (which sold for £460) is believed to be the forty-third machine to have been built. The three Deperdussins which flew in the 1911 Circuit of Europe Race were powered by a 50 hp Gnôme rotary engine, whereas the Collection's machine is powered by a 35 hp

Anzani radial ('Y'-type) engine, producing a top speed of 55 mph. This particular aeroplane was used at Hendon until offered for sale in its damaged condition in 1914. Albert Grimmer, proprietor of the Flitt Motor Co., who also bought the Blériot in the Shuttleworth Collection, acquired the Deperdussin. After repairing both machines he flew them from a polo ground near Bedford. The Blériot and Deperdussin were later placed in storage in a loft above his premises at Ampthill. There they remained until Richard Shuttleworth acquired them in 1935. Although complete, the Deperdussin, like the Blériot, was badly deteriorated and had to be completely rebuilt at Old Warden. The 'Dep' was finally completed in 1937 and was flown by Richard before being stored again during World War Two. The Deperdussin was used in the 1965 film *Those Magnificent Men in their Flying Machines* and it is still capable of making a half circuit of Old Warden when weather conditions are ideal.

◀ Deperdussin cockpit.

Andy Sephton flying the Deperdussin at Old Warden. ▶

1910 Bristol Boxkite

ody's Cathedral. This 100 hp Lycoming-powered Rolls-Royce 0200B powered two-seat reproduction aeroplane was built by F.G. Miles Ltd, and Miles Marine & Structural Plastics Ltd of Shoreham-by-Sea for use (like the Avro Triplane replica) in *Those Magnificent Men in their Flying Machines*. In the film the Boxkite becomes the 'Phoenix Flyer' 'flown' by Orville Newton (played by Stuart Whitman). Miss Patricia Rawnsley (played by Sarah Miles) sometimes accompanies him as passenger. After filming was completed, the Bristol Aeroplane Company purchased one of the replicas and presented it to the Collection in 1966.

The boxkite structure was invented in 1893 by an Australian, Lawrence Hargrave. This simple structure provided good lift and stability, and formed the basis of early aeroplanes such as the Voisin biplane, which in 1907 was modified to improve its performance and handling qualities by Henry Farman (1874–1958), an Englishman living in France. When it appeared in 1909, the Henry Farman III (as it was called) was recognised as a marked improvement over the French machine and became one of the greatest aeroplanes of all time. It had elevators ahead of and behind the mainplanes, a biplane tail, two rudders and a pusher propeller (the replica machine has three rudders because of the small propeller on the 0200 engine). Power was provided by either a 50/60 hp

ENV Gregoire, or a 50 hp, 60 hp or 70 hp Renault engine. At the famous August 1909 Rheims meeting the Boxkite carried off the distance prize with a flight of 112 miles. In the 1910 *Daily Mail* London–Manchester air race, both competitors (Louis Paulhan and Claude Grahame-White) flew improved versions of the Boxkite, which had slightly longer fuselages and extended upper wing spans (34 ft 1 in). Not surprisingly, the Boxkite was copied by many other designers.

No original Boxkite exists. In 1910, however, Boxkites were being built at the rate of two a week and by the end of the year, sixteen had been completed. On 19 February 1910 the Bristol Colonial Aeroplane Company was founded by the entrepreneur millionaire Sir George White. In February 1911 Sir George revealed that the Imperial Russian Army had placed an order for no fewer than eight

machines, the first Government order ever placed with a British aircraft manufacturer. In March that same year, the War Office ordered four examples for British military purposes. The price of the machine at the 1911 Paris Aero Salon was 23,750 francs (£943). Bristol missions, equipped with Boxkites, were sent to Australia, New Zealand and India. The Belgian aviator Christiaens also chose the Boxkite for his tour of Singapore, South Africa and South America. The last survivor, No. 133, was shipped to Australia in January 1913. Australian pilots obtained their certificates as late as 20 October 1915 on this veteran Boxkite.

◀ Boxkite aloft at Old Warden.

1910 Avro Triplane

Originally apprenticed to Lancashire & Yorkshire Railways, Alliott Verdon Roe studied Marine Engineering at King's College, London, and went to sea as an engineer with the South African Mail Company. In 1902 he worked as a draughtsman at Brotherton & Cockers Motor Company. In 1906 Roe became interested in aircraft and he became Secretary of the local aero club. Initially, he worked on the Davidson Gyrocopter and in 1907–08 he built his first biplane, which was hopped at Brooklands.

In 1908–09 he built a triplane under the arches of the Great Eastern Railway at Lea Marshes in Essex. On 13 July 1909 Roe managed a flight of 100 ft to become the first Briton to make a powered flight of any length in an all-British aeroplane. Roe's Triplane, which was driven by a 9 hp motorcycle-type JAP V-twin engine, driving a four-bladed paddle-type propeller, was by its very nature restricted to experimental hops.

Nevertheless, the machine produced remarkable results given its low power output and frail construction. The Triplane IV had an outstanding aspect (span-to-chord) ratio greater than nine to one to minimise induced drag. A control-wheel (turned as in a car) twisted the shape of the outer sections of the two upper sets of wings to provide lateral control through wing warping. It all augured well for the future A.V. Roe company, which was registered in 1910 at Brownfield Mills, Manchester. That same year the company exhibited a Triplane with a price tag of £600 at the Olympia Aero Show.

A.V. Roe went on to construct ever more powerful triplane designs, the most advanced being powered by a 35 hp Green in-line, water-cooled engine, before the company switched in 1911 to the production of biplanes for the British Military Trials of 1912. One of the original Triplanes is exhibited at the Science Museum at South Kensington in London, but its 'engine' is a dummy installation. A replica Avro Triplane is at Brooklands Museum, Weybridge, Surrey. The Avro Triplane owned by the Collection is a superb reproduction, powered by a 1927 105 hp Cirrus Hermes II engine. It was built by the Hampshire Aeroplane Club at Eastleigh, Southampton, for use in the 1965 film *Those Magnificent Men in their Flying Machines*. In the film the dastardly Sir Percy (played by Terry Thomas), who is determined to win the London–Paris air race by fair means or foul, 'flies' the Avro Triplane before its 'demise' aboard a steam train in France as it enters a tunnel! The aeroplane was acquired for the Collection in 1966 and still flies today.

Gordon McClymont in the Avro. Gordon is the chief test pilot at BAe Warton. ◀ ▶

Avro Triplane in the air at Old Warden. ▲

1912 Blackburn

Famous as the oldest genuine original British aeroplane still flying, this 1912 monoplane was bought by Richard Shuttleworth after being discovered in 1938 in semi-crashed condition under a hayrick near Bawtry, where it had lain since 1914. The 50 hp Gnôme rotary engine, with spare parts, was found in a dismantled state in a barrel. The farmer was reluctant to move the hayrick to allow access to the undercarriage so Richard bought the hayrick too! He and W.H.C. 'Billy' Blake removed them to Old Warden on a trailer towed by a 30/98 Vauxhall which Richard drove in his characteristic motor-racing style (at times reaching over 75 mph) despite a lack of braking power!

This aeroplane was one of the first single-seat monoplanes built by Robert Blackburn (one of Britain's pioneer aeroplane designers), and was made for Mr Cyril E. Foggin, who qualified for his Aviator's Certificate at the Blackburn School at Hendon on 19 October 1912. The aeroplane was later acquired by Montague F. Glew who had also learned to fly with the School at the same time.

The Blackburn evolved from the differently powered variants known as 'Mercuries'. One version appeared at the Aero Show Olympia in 1911, priced at £500. A two-seat version was designed for the 1912 British Military Trials but was not ready on time. However, it was the first British aircraft to have an all-metal fuselage.

Richard never saw his Blackburn fly. Restoration began in 1939 and a 50 hp Gnôme, which had previously powered the single-seat Sopwith Type TBP biplane (Harry Hawker's 1914–18 war personal transport) was fitted. The monoplane was not fully restored until 1949, when Group Captain Allen Wheeler flew it on its first post-restoration flight on 25 September at Farnborough. An interesting feature of this aeroplane is a cross-bar, actually a continuation of the wing rear spar, which clamps into position across the pilot's lap after he has taken up his position at the controls. The Blackburn had a close shave during the making of the 1965 film *Those Magnificent Men in their Flying Machines*, almost coming to grief when the German entrant in the film ran out of control on the ground after losing its tail! By 1990 the aeroplane had flown a total of sixteen hours in the air.

Andy Sephton taking off from Old Warden in the Blackburn. ▲

The Blackburn is powered by a 50 hp Gnôme rotary engine. ▶

1915 Avro 504K

n 1912 Roy Chadwick (who later designed the Lancaster bomber) joined A.V. Roe at Brooklands as a draughtsman and their efforts marked a new era in aviation history. The first Avro 500 flew on 8 May 1912. In 1914, new premises were rented at Newton Heath, Manchester. Many of the 8,000 Avro 504s built during 1914–18 were sent to the Western Front for service with the RFC. At first they were used on observation duties, but their potential as bombers was soon realised. Four Avro 504s carried out one of the first bombing raids in the history of aerial warfare in November 1914, when they bombed the Zeppelin works at Friedrichshafen.

However, it is as a trainer that the Avro 504 is best known. HRH Prince Albert (later King George VI) learned to fly on the Avro 504J. In World War One the Avro 504J, which was powered by a 100 hp Gnôme Monosoupape, was recognised as the best training machine in the world, and it served with many overseas air forces in this role. The Avro 504J became the standard equipment of the School of Special Flying at Gosport, Hampshire, and remained in RAF service until September 1921. The Avro 504K, which appeared in 1918, differed from the Avro 504J in having an open-fronted cowling and modified engine-bearers, able to take a variety of engines, including the Monosoupape and Le Rhône engines, 130 hp Clerget, and even the 150 hp Bentley BR-1. The Avro 504K was standard equipment at the Central Flying School and five Flying Training Schools until the mid-1920s, when it was largely replaced by the Lynx-engined 504N.

H5199 was built in 1918 as an Avro 504K and was later civilianised as G-ADEV, modified to an 'N', then returned to a 'K'.

Richard Shuttleworth acquired it in odd circumstances after the operator, Talbot Lehmann, who ran an air circus at Chelmsford, skipped the country leaving many debts unpaid, and the Avro abandoned on a field. At Old Warden the Avro was used to give five-minute pleasure rides for 5s (25p) between Luton and Dunstable. On one occasion Richard Shuttleworth and Squadron Leader 'Jacko' Jackson tried to take off to return to Old Warden, but it failed to get airborne, probably because of an incorrect mixture setting, and it ended up upside down in a field. It won the 1937 Devon Air Race flying at a speed of 103 mph and in 1940 this machine was commandeered for RAF service (as BK892) and used for gliding towing experiments.

H5199 was acquired for the Collection in 1958. Rebuilding and restoration to the original K-standard was undertaken by apprentices at the A.V. Roe Company. The 110 hp Le Rhône radial engine fitted was taken from a damaged Hanriot biplane, which had been acquired on the continent and flown back to the United Kingdom before the Second World War. Work on the aeroplane was completed in time for it to take part in the film *Reach For The Sky*, the life story of Group Captain Douglas Bader.

Avro 504K H5199 being towed out at Old Warden. ▲

Andy Sephton at the controls of H5199 near Old Warden. ▶

1916 Sopwith Pup

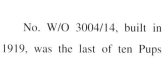

One of the famous stable of Sopwith machines of World War One, the Pup followed the 1½ Strutter and preceded the more famous Triplane. The Pup was powered by an 80 hp Le Rhône engine and armed with a single Vickers gun, mounted centrally atop the fuselage, and fitted with a padded windscreen at its rear end. The Vickers was synchronised to fire through the arc of the propeller by Sopwith-Kauper mechanical interrupter gear. (Some Royal Naval Air Service Pups were fitted with an unsynchronised Lewis gun, the firing position of which was arranged to clear the propeller.) The RNAS ordered the Pup early in 1916 and used many to pioneer the operation of land planes from the decks of aircraft carriers.

The Pup was later adopted by the RFC and from December 1916 was used very effectively as a Scout (fighter) on the Western Front. Although by now the 80 hp Le Rhône-engined machine was slow by the standards of the time, the Pup nevertheless gave a very good account of itself. It was fully aerobatic up to 15,000 ft and was recognised as a superb flying machine, probably the finest on the Western Front. Even Baron von Richtofen was moved to write that, attacked by a Pup, 'we saw immediately that the enemy aeroplane was superior to ours'.

No. W/O 3004/14, built in 1919, was the last of ten Pups converted, in 1925, to two-seat civilianised Doves. Registered G-EBKY, it was owned and flown by D.L. Hollis-Williams, later Chief Engineer of Fairey Aviation. In 1927 it was partially wrecked at Bournemouth as a result of an engine cowling coming adrift just after the aeroplane had taken off from the old Ensbury Park aerodrome. (Incidentally, during a flying display by Bill Bowker at Old Warden on 9 August 1991, the nose and side cowlings became detached and caused superficial damage.) G-EBKY then passed into the hands of C.H. Lowe-Wylde (designer of the BAC Drone) of Rochester Street, Clapham, who operated it from West Malling and flew it regularly until his death at the aerodrome in 1933. It was then purchased by an ex-RFC pilot called Ogilvie and stored at Watford. In 1935 Ogilvie sold it to G.A. Chamberlain for a nominal £45. Chamberlain flew the aeroplane from Marsh Ley's Farm, Kempston, near Bedford, without the benefit of a C of A or a pilot's licence!

Warden Aviation acquired the aeroplane from Chamberlain in 1936 by swopping it for Avro 504K G-ABSN, four barrels of castor oil and a spare set of wings! At Old Warden Richard Shuttleworth had the Dove re-converted almost to a Pup, complete with dummy Vickers machine-gun. Re-conversion was simplified by the fact that the manufacturers had omitted to give the wings the characteristic sweep-back which was normally associated with the Dove. Its first post-restoration flight, in the hands of Allen Wheeler, took place on 26 February 1938. G-EBKY used to fly wearing the serial N5180, which was the number applied to the prototype Pup; but now flies as N6181 Happy of No. 3 Naval Air Squadron.

◀ Sopwith Pup becoming airborne at Old Warden.

Andy Sephton flying the Pup. ▶

1916 Sopwith Triplane

ollowing successful Service Trials with Naval 'A' Fighting Squadron at Furnes in June 1916, production Triplanes began operation with Nos 1 and 8 (Naval) Squadrons in February 1917, and with No. 10 (Naval) Squadron in May that same year. Total deliveries to the RNAS numbered about 140, over 90 of which were built by Sopwith at Kingston-on-Thames to original Admiralty contracts. The remainder were built by subcontractors Clayton & Shuttleworth Ltd (50 examples) based at Lincoln, and Oakley Ltd, Ilford.

The aeroplane enjoyed a remarkable rate of roll and fast climb, qualities appreciated in air combat by the pilots of 'Naval Eight' and 'Naval Ten'. The Triplanes (named *Black Death*, *Black Maria*, *Black Roger*, *Black Prince* and *Black Sheep*) of Flight Sub-Lieutenant Raymond Collishaw's B Flight of 'Naval Ten', laid claim to the destruction of no fewer than 87 German aircraft from May to July 1917. However, the Triplane's career was relatively brief. By November 1917, after just seven months on the Western Front, it was replaced in squadron service by the legendary Sopwith Camel.

Dixie II is the Collection's reproduction Triplane, which was completed by the Northern Aeroplane Workshop on an entirely voluntary basis in 1991. It represents a machine flown by 'Naval 8', many of whose Triplanes were named after wives and sweethearts of its pilots. The Collection requested a colour scheme of a Clayton & Shuttleworth-built Triplane, which has a clear link to today's Shuttleworth Collection. The one chosen was N6290 which was flown by Flight Commanders Arnold and Robert Compston with 'Naval 8'. N6290 was eventually lost on 9 August 1917 while being flown by Flight Sub-Lieutenant Munro. The Collection's machine is powered by an original 130 hp Clerget rotary engine, one of two given to the Collection. *Dixie II*, which first flew, in the hands of John Lewis, on 10 April 1992, was described by the late Sir Thomas Sopwith as a 'late production machine' as opposed to a replica! The Northern Aeroplane Workshop is currently building a Sopwith Camel which will join *Dixie II* at Old Warden in the near future.

Sopwith Triplane speeds past the crowd line. ▲

Andy Sephton aloft in the Triplane. ▶

1916 Bristol M1C

uring 1914–18 the Bristol Colonial Aeroplane Company was responsible for many interesting and innovative aeroplanes, not least the F2b, or 'Bristol Fighter'. One of the company's designers was Scotsman Captain Frank Sowter Barnwell RFC, who in 1915 designed a strong, single-seat, monoplane. Farnborough, however, favoured the more traditional biplane types and had long counselled against monoplane designs, so Barnwell's chances of success in this direction were remote.

Designated M1A (Bristol Type 10), the monoplane had a fully faired fuselage, and shoulder-mounted wings braced by wires from a cabane structure over the cockpit. Power was provided by a 110 hp Clerget engine and a spinner with a large diameter was employed to streamline the installation as much as possible. Barnwell first flew his new monoplane (A5138) in July 1916, achieving a speed of 132 mph, making it faster than the Camel and almost an equal of the SE5a. Four examples were constructed as M1Bs with slight modifications and armed with a single synchronised forward-firing Vickers gun mounted on the port decking.

In September 1916 Freddy Raynham demonstrated the new machine to the Air Staff. Although delightful to fly, the M1C had a high landing speed of 49 mph, and Raynham badly damaged the machine when he misjudged his approach. In any event, the Air Staff considered that the poor pilot field of view downwards made the M1C unsuitable for air combat on the Western Front. RFC pilots had eagerly anticipated the arrival of the fast new machine in squadron service and the outcome, ill-informed as it was, caused consternation. Despite lobbying by Bristol (and cut-outs being made in the wings) the RFC took delivery of only 125 production machines, which were used by training schools in Britain (often as 'instructors' pets', with garish colour schemes) and by two operational units overseas. Each machine was powered by the 110 hp Le Rhône rotary engine, with the Vickers gun being mounted centrally and synchronised by the Constantinesco gear.

The only British-built monoplanes of the Great War, M1Cs served with the Middle East Brigade of the RFC/RAF, equipping No. 72 Squadron in Mesopotamia (now Iraq) in 1917 and No. 150 Squadron at Salonika, operating against the Turks and Bulgars during 1918. No. 72 Squadron archives record that a large group of Kurdish tribesmen allied themselves to the British forces after witnessing a flying display by four of the unit's M1Cs.

On 21 June 1919 G-EAER, an M1C still fitted with its Le Rhône rotary, was the only monoplane entered in the Victory Aerial Derby around London. G-EAER completed the first circuit at just under 100 mph, but on the second lap engine trouble forced its pilot, Major C.H. Chichester-Smith DSO, to return to Hendon.

That same year, Captain Godoy of the Chilean Air Force flew an M1C (one of six supplied to the Chilean Government in lieu of two battleships) from Santiago, Chile, to Mendoza, Argentina, to make the first aerial crossing of the Andes. It entailed climbing to 13,000 ft to clear the Uspallata Pass. On 4 April 1919 Lieutenant Cortinez, a student pilot, went one better, making the same flight in an M1C at night!

C4918, a late reproduction M1C powered by a 110 hp nine-cylinder Le Rhône rotary engine manufactured by the Northern Aeroplane Workshop, was built for the Collection in 1997. The colour scheme is the standard Middle East PC12 red-brown. John Lewis flew Don Cashmore's replica M1C before it became a permanent exhibit at the RAF Museum. He compared the ground handling with a bar of wet soap and, furthermore, said that 'the cockpit access requires the skills of Houdini'.

Bristol M1C resplendent in Middle East red-brown scheme, characteristic of the colours worn in 'Mesops' in 1917. ▶

1917 Bristol F2b

hip Shape and Bristol Fashion. The F2b, or the 'Biff' or 'Brisfit' as it was affectionately known, was designed by Captain Frank Barnwell RFC and L.G. Frise. It was armed with a Vickers machine-gun synchronised to fire through the arc of the propeller with Constantinesco gear for the pilot and either single or twin Lewis guns on a Scarff ring for the observer. Two 112 lb bombs could be carried below the wings. The F2b could take various powerplants, such as the Hispano-Suiza, Siddeley Puma, Wolseley Viper or the Sunbeam Arab, but its greatest engine power, in the autumn of 1917, was provided by the 275 hp Rolls-Royce Falcon III, which gave 125 mph at sea level and 108 mph at 13,000 ft. (The early side radiators were later deleted to improve the field of view from the cockpit.) The fuselage was mounted high between the wings, giving its pilot and observer an excellent view above and below the top wing, and the type was first used in an armed reconnaissance role.

The F2b flew for the first time in September 1916. On 8 March 1917, No. 48 Squadron, commanded by Captain Leefe-Robinson VC, flew the first production models to France. It was used operationally for the first time on 5 April 1917, during the spring offensive on the Western Front. No. 48 Squadron suffered early heavy losses as German pilots exploited the F2b crews' poor defensive tactics, attacking from below and directly astern.

The RFC soon learned to use the F2b in an offensive role, as despite its weight and size the Bristol Fighter was equally as fast and manoeuvrable as the German single-seat machines and could dive faster than any other type on the Western Front. In a dog-fight the pilot learned to fly it like a single-seater, using his forward-firing Vickers machine-gun in the manner of a fighting scout while the observer guarded his rear with single or twin Lewis guns. In this role the 'Brisfit' proved a powerful and effective weapon and it developed into the finest two-seat fighter of World War One.

By the end of World War One Bristol Fighters equipped fourteen squadrons and some 3,100 had been built. The type saw widespread post-war service as the RAF's standard Army-Co-operative aircraft in Ireland and Germany until 1922, and on the Northwest Frontier of India and in Iraq until 1932 when it was finally superseded by the Fairey Gordon. Bristol Fighters also equipped eight foreign air forces. When production finally ceased in December 1926, a further 1,369 models had been built.

D8096, the Collection machine, was built at Brislington Carriage Works, Bristol, in 1918 and was sold on 18 June to the Air Board, priced at £1,175 without an engine. It was issued to No. 208 Squadron in Turkey in 1923. In about 1936 the aircraft was acquired at a disposal sale by Captain C.P.B. Ogilvie, who stored the aeroplane at Primrose Garages, Watford, with the intention of restoring it. Although the civil registration G-AEPH was allotted, the ex-RFC pilot never

Andrew Belling gets to grips with the Bristol F2b. Andrew trained as an aircraft apprentice engineer at Farnborough and worked at the Collection until 1998. ▲

Gordon McClymont aloft in the Bristol Fighter near Old Warden. ▶

realised this ambition. The F2b was discovered stored in a shed at Elstree aerodrome in 1949. It was accepted by the Shuttleworth Trust together with a spare engine, a stock of spares, various other parts and the Hucks Starter. By courtesy of Lord Hives the engines were overhauled by Rolls-Royce. Restoration of the aeroplane structure was carried out by the then Bristol Aeroplane Company.

▲ The Hucks Starter came from the same source as the Bristol Fighter and was rebuilt and restored for the Collection by the de Havilland Aircraft Co., which is believed to have been responsible for the conversion of a large number of Model 'T' Ford cars to this role.

◀ Bristol F2b being flown by Gordon McClymont. ▶

1917 Royal Aircraft Factory SE5a

The SE5a, developed from the SE (Scout Experimental) 5, was one of the finest single-seat fighters of World War One and the favourite mount of many British aces. The SE5a flew for the first time on 22 November 1916 and No. 56 Squadron was the first to receive the type, at London Colney, Hertfordshire, on 13 March 1917. The following month No. 56 Squadron was posted to France and became the first of fourteen squadrons to use the type on the Western Front. Eventually the type equipped twenty-four RFC and RAF squadrons in France, Palestine, Macedonia, Mesopotamia and the United Kingdom. It also equipped one squadron of the Australian Flying Corps and two squadrons of the US Air Service.

A very powerful and robust fighter, the SE5a owed its combat success to a combination of speed and its stability as a gun platform. The armament consisted of one fixed, synchronised forward-firing Vickers machine-gun and one Lewis machine-gun on a Foster mounting above the top wing. There was provision for four 25 lb Cooper bombs under the wings. Power was provided by either a 200 hp or 220 hp Hispano-Suiza, a 200 hp Wolseley W4A Viper, a 200 hp Wolseley Adder, or a 200 hp Sunbeam Arab engine.

A total of 5,205 SE5/SE5as was built. Among the most famous pilots who flew the SE5a were Major Edward 'Mick' Mannock VC of No. 74 'Tiger' Squadron and Major James McCudden VC. Mannock was killed on 26 July 1918 when a German rifleman's bullet hit his petrol tank but his confirmed total of seventy-three remained unbeaten by any other British ace during World War One. McCudden's total of fifty-seven victories made him the fourth highest scoring British ace by the end of World War One. He was killed in a flying accident in France on 9 July 1918.

F904 (G-EBIA), one of fifty that came on to the civil market after May 1920, was used by Major Jack Savage's Skywriting Company in 1924. This aeroplane, less the engine, was found hanging from the roof of the flight shed at what was then the Armstrong-Whitworth Aircraft factory at Whitley, near Bagington, Coventry. The Royal Aircraft Establishment at Farnborough was anxious to have a specimen of this Royal Aircraft Factory (later RAE, now DERA) designed aeroplane available for display so they agreed to restore it for the Shuttleworth Collection. The restoration, by apprentices and staff at RAE Farnborough, began in 1957 and the SE5a flew again on 4 August 1959 in the hands of Allen Wheeler. Following problems with the Hispano-Suiza engine it was replaced in 1975 by a 200 hp Wolseley Viper V-eight engine found in America.

Cockpit and gun installation on the SE5a. ▲

Chris Huckstep aloft in the SE5a. ▶

◄ This view of the SE5a banking away reveals this famous fighter's powerful and robust construction, which made it such a formidable adversary over the trenches in World War One.

Chris Huckstep at the controls of the SE5a closes in in a manner reminiscent of the fighter's role on the Western Front. From this range its menacing appearance must have struck terror in the hearts of even the most battle-hardened enemy rear gunners. ▶

1917 Luft-Verkehrs-Gesellschaft LVG CVI

LVG CVI 7198/18 (/18 refers to the year of manufacture), a reconnaissance and short-distance light bomber, was captured almost complete, apart from instruments and armament, at the end of World War One. It was powered by a 230 hp Benz upright in-line engine. It was armed with a single fixed Spandau gun off-set to the starboard side of the cockpit, firing forward through the arc of the propeller, and one moveable Parabellum gun operated from the rear cockpit.

Believed to have been assembled from two or even three different captured machines, this LVG was subsequently flown by the A&AEE (Aeroplane and Armament Experimental Establishment) at Martlesham Heath, Suffolk. Stored for many years by the Historical Branch of the Air Ministry (now Air Historical Branch), the LVG was loaned to the Science Museum but it was not put on display. This aeroplane was flown at the 1937 Hendon Air Pageant when it appeared in mock combat with a Sopwith Triplane, a Bristol Fighter and an SE5a. Almost thirty years later it was acquired for the Collection on extended loan from the MoD and patiently restored to flying condition at Old Warden. The aircraft is now owned by the RAF Museum in Hendon, and the intention is that the LVG will go on display at a new World War One hall, but an agreement with the Shuttleworth trustees means that the LVG will fly at least until 2008 before being grounded.

▲ LVG and SE5a in formation. Note the German machine's Parabellum or Mondraggen machine-gun on its moveable mounting in the rear cockpit for the observer. A single synchronised Spandau machine-gun was bolted to the fuselage and operated by the pilot with a Bowden wire control.

▶ Tony Haig-Thomas, one of the Shuttleworth Trust's two main directors, taxying the LVG at Old Warden. Tony joined the RAF straight from school at 18. In 1966 he competed in the World Aerobatic Championship at Moscow with a Zlin. He flies his own Avenger, Harvard and Cub, as well as many of the Collection's aircraft.

1921 English Electric Wren

No, English Electric did not always manufacture Mach 2 Lightnings! Everyone has to start somewhere, and in 1922 Mr W.O. Manning FRAeS, the then chief designer of this world famous company's Aircraft Division, came up with the Wren to meet an Air Ministry Specification which called for an ultra-light training aircraft capable of up to thirty minutes' flight duration. (On reflection, this was not too dissimilar to that of the Lightning's duration!)

The Wren (J6973) was powered by a 3 hp overhead valve 398 cc flat-twin ABC motorcycle-type engine, specially adapted for fitting to an aircraft, which drove a two-bladed mahogany tractor screw just 3 ft 6 in in diameter. The fuel tank capacity was an equally modest one gallon. The maximum speed was 50 mph but it could fly quite well at little more than 20 mph. In 1923 one of these machines won the *Daily Mail* Light Aeroplane Contest at Lympne, Kent, when it flew 87.5 miles on its gallon of fuel. On other occasions flights of over 100 miles were made using the same amount of fuel, and a height of 1,200 ft was also achieved by a Wren.

Only the prototype and three other Wrens were built. No. 4 (c/n 3!) was presented to the Collection by R. H. Grant of Dumfries and rebuilt by the English Electric Company using many components from No. 3 (c/n 4!) held by the Science Museum. On completion No. 4 was flown at Warton in January 1957 and presented at the RAeS (Royal Aeronautical Society) Garden Party later that year. It was extensively refurbished in 1980 and rejoined the Collection early in 1981.

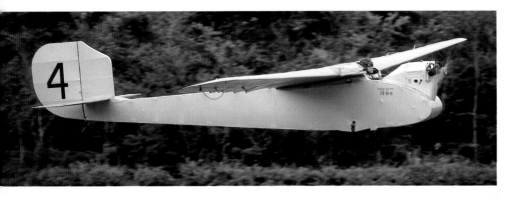

▲ The 3 hp 398 cc ABC motorcycle-type engine to the fore on the Wren. In its original form the engine could be run up to 4,000 rpm but is now limited to 2,700 rpm.

◀ Andy Sephton airborne ('just') in the Wren at Old Warden. The machine is perfectly controllable at speeds of little more than 20 mph.

Andy Sephton taxies the Wren past the crowd line at Old Warden. ▶

1923 de Havilland DH53 Humming Bird

First in the long line of famous de Havilland light aircraft, the DH53 was built for the *Daily Mail* light aeroplane trials (which were instigated by the Air Ministry), at Lympne in October 1923. The wings were of two-spar construction, fabric-covered with differential ailerons. Bracing was in the form of solid spruce V struts, in compression, attached to the top longerons. Engineer and author Nevil Shute Norway, who recalled the Humming Bird in his book *Slide Rule*, designed the DH53's small wooden propeller.

Like the Wren, the two identical prototypes were powered by a motorcycle engine, in this case a 750 cc Douglas twin-cylinder. *Humming Bird* was owned by the company and piloted by test pilot Hubert Broad, while *Sylvia II* was owned by Alan S. Butler, Chairman of the de Havilland Company (from February 1923 – June 1950), and was flown by Major Harold Hemming. Both pilots superbly demonstrated the aeroplanes to their full potential. Hemming in fact covered 59.3 miles on one gallon of petrol, and Broad performed loops and rolls never before seen on such a small aeroplane. However, the DH53 was undeniably underpowered and the Douglas engine proved so unreliable that the aeroplanes failed to win any of the prizes on offer.

Upon return to Stag Lane the troublesome Douglas was replaced on the first prototype (now registered G-EBHX) by the 26 hp 697 cc Tomtit, an inverted V-twin manufactured by Burney and Blackburne Engines Ltd of Bookham, Surrey. In preparation for its flight by Sir Alan Cobham to the 1923 Brussels Aero Show, the fuel capacity was increased from its original two gallons by the installation of an extra tank in the form of a streamlined headrest. At the same time, miniature rubber-in-compression units were used to replace the unsatisfactory bungee shock absorbers previously fitted. G-EBHX also received the new name *L'OISEAU-MOUCHE* for the show. During the flight on 8 December the new Tomtit engine produced 3,000 rpm, which is reputed to be the reason for the DH53 being called the 'Humming Bird'. Cobham called at Croydon and Lympne before setting out on the 150-mile final leg across the Channel, taking four hours to cover the distance. On his return flight, a strong headwind slowed the DH53 to such a degree that Cobham was actually overtaken by a train, so he decided to land and have the aeroplane shipped home. The following year Cobham finished eighth at the Grosvenor Trophy Race at Lympne in this machine, flying at 67.35 mph.

The twelve DH53 production versions built were fitted with the Tomtit, as well as the horizontally-opposed twins, the Bristol Cherub and, alternatively, the 34 hp 1.1 litre ABC Scorpion flat-twin. The largest order for DH53s was placed by the Air Ministry, which received eight Tomtit-engined aircraft for communications and practice flying. The first six (J7268–J7273) made their public debut together in the race between Air Ministry Directorates at the 1925 Hendon RAF Display. The two other RAF machines were experimentally air-launched from the R-33 airship late in 1925. After the flight the Humming Birds were hooked back onto the airship. In 1927 the eight DH53s were put up for sale on the civil market.

Reconditioned by students (that included the Collection's current Chief Engineer, Chris Morris), at the DH Technical School at Hatfield, after passing through several civil owners, the first post-restoration flight occurred on 4 August 1960 in the hands of DH test pilot Chris Capper. It was delivered to Old Warden on 1 September, painted in the colours it wore for the Lympne competition.

▲ Bill Bowker makes the DH53's ABC Scorpion engine hum while on the chocks at Old Warden.

1924 Hawker Cygnet

gly Ducking. The Cygnet was Sydney Camm's first design for Hawker, and was also the company's entry for the Light Aeroplane Competition organised by the Royal Aero Club in 1924, for which the Air Ministry offered prizes to the value of £3,000. Two Cygnets, G-EBMB, powered by a 34 hp Anzani, and G-EBJH, powered by a 34 hp ABC Scorpion, were built for the competition (with entry numbers 14 and 11), and finished third and fourth respectively. In 1925 G-EBMB won the 100-mile International Handicap Race at the RAeC (Royal Aero Club) Lympne meeting. Both Cygnets were re-engined with the 34 hp Bristol Cherub for the 1926 Lympne Light Plane Competition. G-EBMB, flown by P.W.S. Bulman, won the *Daily Mail*'s £3,000 first prize. G-EBJH finished second. In 1972 G-EBMB went on display at the RAF Museum, Hendon.

G-CAMM, a reproduction aeroplane built by Don Cashmore, was loaned to

the Collection in 1996. It is powered by a relatively modern American-built 35 hp Mosler flat-twin based on a pair of Volkswagen cylinders mated to a new crank and crankcase. It is of similar configuration and horsepower to the original twin-cylinder Anzani and 34 hp Bristol Cherub III flat-twin installed in one of the prototypes (the other was originally powered by an ABC Scorpion, but both were later re-engined with Cherubs).

What is it like to fly? Pilot Rob Millichip said: 'Summed up in a single word, lovely! *But*, quite demanding . . . and tricky to taxi in a dignified manner. Although extremely light, and very low powered, its ability to cope with a comparatively stiff breeze has proved very useful, allowing it to be flown when other, rather less controllable machines have been grounded by the weather.'

This aircraft is privately owned but based with the Shuttleworth Collection

▲ A 35 hp Mosler flat-twin based on a pair of Volkswagen cylinders, mated to a new crank and crankcase is used to power the Cygnet.

HAWKER CYGNET

DESIGNED BY SYDNEY CAMM, 1924

▲Rob Millinship aloft in the Cygnet.

1924 de Havilland DH51 *Miss Kenya*

Kenyan Miss. Kenya, the land of the Kikuyu, the Nandi, and the Masai, is an unpredictable country full of breathtaking sights where one can zoom low, like Redford and Streep in *Out of Africa*, over the pink blanket of flamingo-populated Lake Nakuru, or brush the slopes of the Ngong Hills and the vast tracts of the Serengeti and the Molo-places where Beryl Markham once flew her Avro Avian.

The first aircraft to be registered in Kenya was G-EBIR. This two-bay, plywood fuselage and fabric-covered machine accommodated either two people and luggage, or three people, and was equipped with a sliding top fuselage fairing to adjust the layout. The DH51 design originated in 1923 with the release of a batch of war-surplus air-cooled 90 hp Royal Aircraft Factory 1A heavy, single-ignition air-cooled engines. G-EBIM, the DH51 prototype, flew for the first time on 1 July 1924 fitted with a 1A engine. After G-EBIM made four force landings in a mid-1920s King's Cup Air Race between London and Newcastle because of ignition problems, it was decided to replace

the troublesome 1A with a more suitable engine. The French war-surplus eight-cylinder Renault 80 hp engine was being developed for civil use and Major Frank Halford's Aircraft Disposal Company (Airdisco) increased the engine's output to 120 hp.

In 1925, G-EBIQ and G-EBIR, were constructed, fitted with the Airdisco-Renault engine. Both aircraft were test-flown by Captain Geoffrey de Havilland. G-EBIR received its initial C of A on 21 September 1925 and was purchased by John Carberry, a coffee bean farmer in Kenya. The DH51 arrived at Seramai in March 1926 after making the last leg of the journey by ox cart! She was re-assembled and Carberry gave the DH51 its first test flight around the Nyeri district on 12 April. Its ability to climb out of small landing strips at 580 ft a minute and its range of 560 miles at 80 mph cruise made it an ideal companion in the treacherous terrain. Once airborne Carberry skirted the snow-capped 13,000 ft Aberdares and 17,058 ft high Mount Kenya.

On 28 March 1928 a syndicate headed by Tom Campbell-Black bought G-EBIR from Carberry. On 10 September the DH51, now called *Miss Kenya*, became the first aircraft to be registered in Kenya (G-KAA). On 3 January 1929 the registration was changed to VP-KAA under the new colonial system. *Miss Kenya* enjoyed many adventures in the hands of several owners. On 29 May 1951, on delivery to Eastleigh for presentation to the RAF, a heavy landing broke the undercarriage and caused damage to the starboard wing. *Miss Kenya* was hangared until late in 1954 when a complete reconstruction was undertaken. *Miss Kenya* emerged as good as new in September 1955.

On 4 June 1965 she was dismantled for shipment to England aboard a Blackburn Beverley. The Shuttleworth Trust took charge of its preservation and on 14 July 1970 the aircraft was received at the Army Apprentice College REME at Avlonfield where *Miss Kenya* was rebuilt. Meanwhile, Rolls-Royce at Leavesden overhauled the engine. On 15 March 1973 *Miss Kenya*, with Air Commodore Allen Wheeler at the controls, made her first post-restoration flight at the Hawker Siddeley Aviation airfield at Chester. On 23 March at Hatfield test pilots W.P.I. Fillingham and John Cunningham each made fifteen-minute flights in *Miss Kenya*. Two days later, Desmond Penrose of the Shuttleworth Collection made the first flight in *Miss Kenya* at Old Warden.

Miss Kenya is the only surviving DH51 example in the world. Although very popular and docile, the DH51 proved rather large for the average owner's needs and only three were built. ▶

1928 de Havilland DH60X Hermes Moth

t is thought that the name 'Moth' originated from Captain Geoffrey de Havilland's boyhood interest in lepidopterology. The Moth has become one of the most successful light aircraft in aviation history. Much of its early success was due not just to the superb single-bay biplane design, but also to the lightweight yet economical Cirrus upright, in-line engine, which was specially designed by Major Frank B. Halford of Airdisco. Halford created this engine (derived from the old 80 hp Renault) by virtue of removing four of the eight cylinders from the 120 hp V-type engine and mating them to a new crankcase. The result was a 60 hp engine that weighed just 290 lb.

Geoffrey de Havilland flew the first Moth (G-EBKT) on 22 February 1925 at Stag Lane Aerodrome, Edgware, Middlesex. Just three months later, on 29 May, Alan Cobham flew the prototype 1,000 miles from Croydon to Zurich in a day. From then on the aircraft's reputation was assured. The Lancashire Aero Club at Woodford, first of the five Moth clubs that were established, took delivery of its first Moth (G-EBLR) on 21 July 1925 when it was delivered by Alan Cobham. On 29 August 1925 the eighth Moth built, G-EBLV, was accepted by the club. Now owned by BAe, it is the oldest Moth flying anywhere.

DH60 Moths were built under licence in Australia and Finland. They were variously engined with the Cirrus I, II, III, Cirrus Hermes I and the 75 hp Armstrong-Siddeley Genet I radial, to produce the Genet Moth. By 1926 the Moth had almost become a victim of its own success and demand now outstripped Cirrus engine production. Geoffrey de Havilland therefore looked at manufacturing a new engine. It was one which was to revolutionise the DH60 series. Major Halford designed the Gipsy I, rated at 100 hp at 2,100 rpm, and the first engine ran in July 1927. DH60X G-EBQH, the first production Gipsy-powered Moth, was one of three Gipsy-powered Moths entered in the 1928 King's Cup Air Race. One of the production DH60X Moths (G-EBTD) was flown with only routine maintenance for 600 hours after being sealed by AID (Airdisco) between 29 December 1928 and 24 September 1929. On completion of the successful trial, in which the aircraft flew 51,000 miles, only £7 2s 11d had to be spent on replacement parts.

In 1932 Richard Shuttleworth inherited his father's and Uncle Alfred's fortunes, which, combined, exceeded £2 million. On 14 February he made his first solo flights from Brooklands in DH60X Cirrus Moth G-EBWD, his first aeroplane, which he had bought from Brooklands School of Flying for £300 on 21 January. G-EBWD is also the aircraft in which Richard's mother made her first flight, as a passenger. It was built in 1928 and was originally powered by a 85 hp Cirrus II engine. In 1933 the engine was replaced by the 105 hp Hermes II at Old Warden, where the aircraft has become unique as it has been based at the same airfield for longer than any other aeroplane in history.

DH60X G-EBWD was built in 1928 and does not seem to have aged at all. ▲

Trevor Roche aloft in G-EBWD, the first aeroplane purchased by Richard Shuttleworth, in 1932. ▶

1928 de Havilland DH60G Gipsy Moth

Wandering Gipsy. Public adulation of Moths was fired by a series of long-distance records, the most famous of which was undoubtedly Amy Johnson's solo flight to Australia in DH60G Gipsy Moth G-AAAH *Jason* (5–24 May 1930). (*Jason* is on display in the Science Museum, Kensington, London.) In 1930 Francis Chichester, in G-AAKK *Madam Elijah*, became the first man to complete the England to Australia journey in a Moth. Fitted with floats in New Zealand in 1931, the Moth was used by Chichester in his epic navigation and location of the tiny Norfolk and Lord Howe Islands where he landed *en route* to Australia. John Grierson flew G-AAJP *Rouge et Noir* to Lahore, India, in 1930, to Baghdad in 1931, and to Moscow in 1932. In 1933, he attached floats to G-AAJP and flew from Brough to Iceland.

As in the case of the highly dependable Cirrus which powered the DH60, it was the Gipsy engine that formed the reliable core of the DH60G. The 'G' retained the delightful control characteristics of earlier Moths but had a higher wing loading. G-EBYZ, one of fourteen Moths entered in the 1928 King's Cup Air Race, was flown by W.L. Hope, who won the competition with an average speed of 105 mph. On 25 July 1928 Captain Geoffrey de Havilland flew G-AAAA to a record 19,980 ft, and during 16–17 August Hubert Broad in G-EBWV remained aloft over Stag Lane for 24 hours.

G-ABAG (c/n 1259) was built at Stag Lane in 1930 and registered to Bentley Motors Ltd. Before the Second World War the aeroplane was owned by four other owners and it was also loaned to the Stage and Screen Aero Club.

During this time Ralph Richardson learned to fly on G-ABAG. When war broke out in Europe in 1939 G-ABAG, or the 'Bagmoth' as it is known, was put into storage. In 1950 it was used at Perth, Scotland, and subsequently owned by brothers Douglas and Peter Hull. They sold G-ABAG to the Strathtay Aero Club and after it crashed, the Gipsy was returned to the Hull brothers. When Douglas Hull died his widow presented this fine aircraft to the Collection in the summer of 1977.

Dodge Bailey aloft in the 'Bagmoth'. G-ABAG, star of stage and screen, with a pedigree to match. ▶

1928 Hawker Tomtit

ood gives way to metal. When the time came to replace the veteran Avro 504N RAF trainer in the late 1920s, the Air Ministry laid down two preconditions. The new machine was to be designed around the air-cooled 150 hp Armstrong-Siddeley Mongoose five-cylinder radial engine and the airframe was to be of all-metal construction. The Tomtit, which appeared in 1928, and the Mongoose-engined Avro Trainer (forerunner of the Tutor) were the two types selected for evaluation.

Although the Tomtit proved a delightful aeroplane to fly and embodied features not previously fitted to an elementary training aircraft, only twenty-five examples were produced between November 1928 and 1931. In June 1932 the Avro Trainer was selected as an Avro 504N replacement. From 1929 to 1932 Tomtits equipped No. 3 FTS at Grantham, and the type was also used by the Central Flying School at Wittering. A few Tomtits were used on communications duties by No. 24 Squadron at Northolt, where one was often flown by HRH the Prince of Wales (the late Duke of Windsor). The Prince flew one of the two Tomtits entered in the 1930 King's Cup Air Race.

In 1935 the last Tomtits were offered for sale to the civil market. K1786, the last production aircraft and the only surviving Tomtit, became G-AFTA. During World War Two it was used as a 'hack' by Alex Henshaw of pre-war Mew Gull fame, who temporarily fitted a Spitfire windscreen. After the war G-AFTA was sold for £250 to Goodhew Aviation of Kidlington, Oxford, remaining there until 1949. It was often used by R.G. Stafford Allen for glider towing. In 1949 G-AFTA was acquired by Squadron Leader Neville Duke, the famous Hawker chief test pilot, who flew it at several flying meetings. Hawker Aircraft purchased G-AFTA in 1950 to form the Hawker house triumvirate with the Hurricane and Hart, before it was presented to the Shuttleworth Collection in September 1959.

In 1967 G-AFTA was repainted by Hawker Siddeley at Dunsfold from a dark blue and gold scheme to its original RAF markings. In May 1985 at the Mildenhall Air Fete, shortly after refurbishment had been completed, the Tomtit was badly damaged in a landing accident which removed the undercarriage and destroyed the propeller. During an engine run following its restoration, the propeller was found to be flexing out of true. Investigation revealed that this was caused by harmonic vibration between the engine and propeller. Finally, in 1992, an order was placed with Hoffmann Propellers of Germany for a new propeller. The hub was made from compressed beech veneers and spliced with spruce laths towards the tips. The blades were covered with a carbon fibre and epoxy coating with an integral leading edge. The Tomtit flew again on 25 June 1992, the propeller problems cured.

◄ Trevor Roche at the controls of the Tomtit high over Bedfordshire on a summer's day.

One can almost hear the air-cooled 150 hp Mongoose five-cylinder radial purr as Trevor Roche closes on the camera ship near Old Warden. ►

◀ Restoration of the Tomtit, like all the aircraft in the Collection, is so perfect that this view with the backdrop of a breathtaking cloudscape, could easily have been taken in the 1930s.

1929 Parnall Elf

ream and Green. The Elf was the last of a series of light aeroplanes designed by Harold Bolas and produced by George Parnall of Bristol. It appeared for the first time in 1929 and was exhibited at the Olympia Aero Show that same year. This two-seat light biplane was powered by a 105 hp Cirrus Hermes four-cylinder upright, in-line engine, which gave this sturdy machine a top speed of 116 mph. Designed for straightforward maintenance in the private and club market, many of the Elf's features were nevertheless unorthodox. The wings were heavily staggered and placed further forward on the fuselage than was the norm, so that both seats were behind the wings to effect easier escape in an emergency. To prevent the centre of gravity being too far aft, the wings (which could be folded) were given a pronounced sweep-back. The wing bracing was also unusual in that instead of vertical interplane struts and streamline wire bracing, the wings were entirely strut-braced, the struts and wing spars forming a Warren girder structure. Unusually, the twenty-three-gallon petrol tank was carried in the fuselage and a pump was used to raise the supply to a small header tank atop the upper wing centre-section, where the fuel was gravity-fed to the engine.

Though undoubtedly a very promising design, Elfs retailed at between £875 and £890, and only three were constructed. G-AAFH and G-AAIO were lost in flying accidents in 1934. Only G-AAIN, which first flew in June 1932, survives today. Before the war it was owned by Lord Apsley at Badminton. After storage during World War Two, G-AAIN was based at Fairoaks and was acquired in a non-flying condition by the Collection in July 1951. In 1972 the Elf was loaned to the Historic Aircraft Museum at Southend before being restored to flying condition at Old Warden by two former apprentices. G-AAIN, in its beautiful cream and green livery, made its first public flying appearance in August 1980.

▲ Chris Huckstep at the controls of G-AAIN near Old Warden.

◀ An innovative aircraft in many respects, the Elf's upper wing is in the line of sight of the pilot
to give maximum reduction in field of view.

▶ Both seats in the Elf were placed behind the wings to allow easier evacuation in the event of an emergency.

1929 Comper Swift

Angel From Assam. Designed by Flight Lieutenant Nicholas Comper in 1929, the single-seat, high-wing CLA7 Swift monoplane evolved from the CLA3, Comper's third design for the Cranwell Light Aeroplane Club. The '7' was built in 1931–32 and was the only aircraft to enter production with The Comper Aircraft Co. Ltd at Hooton Park Aerodrome in Cheshire. G-AARX, the prototype, was powered by a 35 hp ABC Scorpion engine, but the first of the production models were powered by a 50 hp Salmson AD9 engine. The Swift was designed as a machine capable of a high performance, yet safe in the hands of a novice. This latter point was obviously necessary as it was impossible to have dual instruction, and its low price made it an attractive proposition for the pilot who could not afford to spend much time on larger machines. The wings, which were made to fold, were at pilot's eye-level so that one could see both above and below them. The aeroplane was constructed of wood and steel.

In 1931 a Swift piloted by Mr Butler made a record-breaking flight from England to Australia, and in 1932 and 1933 Swifts came second in the King's Cup Air Race. In the 1933 King's Cup Air Race two other Swifts made the fastest times of the day.

Several models of the Swift were manufactured to suit various purposes. The standard type with a Pobjoy engine of 75 hp was for the private owner and had a cockpit and a small luggage locker. Another type was similar, except that it had a large locker for the carriage of mail or freight. Three Special Swifts intended for high speed were fitted with an inverted Gipsy engine of 120/130 hp. Altogether, some 41 Swifts were built.

G-ACTF, a scarlet and white Pobjoy-engined Swift, built in 1932, was acquired for the Collection in 1996. Originally, it was owned by Alban H. Yusef Ali, an Anglo-Indian civil servant who was responsible for inspecting tea plantations in Assam. Ali had learned to fly at Cramlington, Newcastle, in 1929. After shipment of the Swift to Assam in October 1932, Ali registered his £550 purchase as VT-ADO. In February 1933 the proud new owner competed in the Viceroy's Trophy Race (the Indian equivalent of the King's Cup Air Race) at Delhi and *Scarlet Angel* covered the 700-mile course at an average speed of 124 mph, the second fastest time of the day. Two other Swifts competed in the same race. The Pobjoy-engined G-ABWE was flown by Richard Shuttleworth, who retired with a broken oil feed, while the all-white Gipsy-engined G-ACBY, also owned by Shuttleworth, was flown by Flying Officer George C. Stead and made the fastest time of 153 mph.

Ali also attempted a flight from Calcutta to Heston in 1933. Ali got as far as Abu Sueir in Egypt when the Pobjoy engine, consumed by sand, stopped for good. Badly damaged, VT-ADO was crated up and completed the journey to England by sea, whereupon it was purchased by Airspeed test pilot George Errington, who rebuilt it and reregistered it G-ACTF. Tango Foxtrot later passed to Ron E. Clear of Christchurch, Dorset. During his ownership it was modified for the 1950 *Daily Express* Race with a sliding hood and streamlined wheel spats. It was placed fifth and also set an FAI Class record of 141 mph. G-ACTF was later owned by Captain Alan Chalkley of Blackbushe, a British Airways Boeing 747 pilot.

G-ACTF, the scarlet and white Pobjoy-engined Swift, built in 1932, was acquired for the Collection in 1996. ▶

1930 Granger Archæopteryx

Suffering Pterodactyls! Tailless aeroplanes are among the most unaerodynamic of aircraft and the single Archæopteryx built by R.F.T. and R.J.T. Granger, lace manufacturers by trade, must surely rank as one of the weirdest ultra-lights of all time. Perhaps the Archæopteryx's one and only claim to fame is that it was one of the first tailless tractor types and was a forerunner of the swept-wing types in service today.

The Granger brothers designed the tailless wonder with help from C.H. Latimer-Needham, designer of the Luton light aeroplanes and architect of the Westland-Hill Pterodactyl in 1926. The Archæopteryx had swept-back wings but no elevators or tailplane – although it did have a fin and rudder. Full-chord elevons at the wingtips, hinged near the leading edge, provided control in both roll and pitch. Power was provided by a 32 hp Bristol Cherub I flat twin which drove a small two-bladed propeller. Petrol was gravity-fed from a five-gallon tank in the fuselage (later the Collection modified it and relocated it to the wing centre-section). The basic wing structure was completed in September 1927 but the Archæopteryx was not ready to fly until October 1930, when it took to the air at Hucknall, near Nottingham. It was flown for six years (1930–36). During flight it was essential that its speed never dipped below 50 mph as it could not be allowed to enter the stall.

At first, the aeroplane did not require a C of A but in 1932 the regulations changed and the Grangers' creation was registered G-ABXL. In 1937 G-ABXL was grounded and it was stored for thirty years before being loaned to the Collection on 28 April 1967. Restored to flying condition at Old Warden, G-ABXL was flown again in June 1971. Many years ago the Collection pushed the Archæopteryx to 105 mph in a shallow dive. Just as the dinosaurs are, those occasions are now extinct! When the Archæopteryx has made appearances on flying days it was taxied only, although the process that will see it in the air again soon, is underway.

Most visitors to the ever-popular Shuttleworth flying days have only ever seen the curious little Archæopteryx taxi past during displays but the Collection has already begun the process that will see the 32 hp machine fly once again. Curiously, the throttle lever is on the outside of the fuselage and a positive rate of climb could be obtained only if the pilot's arms and elbows were kept inside the tiny cockpit. ▶

This aircraft is privately owned but based with the Shuttleworth Collection

1931 Desoutter 1

The Desoutter Mk I Coupé monoplane was based on the Dutch-designed Koolhoven FK41 and went into British production at Croydon in 1930. FK41s built on the continent had appeared in the United Kingdom a year earlier. Twenty-eight Desoutter 1s were built in this country powered by a 115 hp Cirrus Hermes II engine and a further thirteen much modified Mk 2s used the D. H. Gipsy III engine. Nineteen machines were bought by the National Flying Services for use on instructional, taxi and pleasure flying work. Two others were operated by the British Red Cross Society on ambulance duties from Croydon Airport and Woodford. One was flown to New Zealand where it continued to be operated commercially for twenty years. Another was flown in Northern Rhodesia on pleasure flights and charter work for several years.

G-AAPZ, one of three owned for a time by Richard Shuttleworth and his Warden Aviation Company, was registered in 1931 and operated by National Flying Services at Hanworth. It was flown in the 1934 King's Cup Air Race by Don Ayre, who finished in fourth place with an average speed of 115.89 mph, a remarkable performance. Richard Shuttleworth acquired this aircraft in 1935

and had it modified to take a Menasco C-4 Pirate engine. In World War Two G-AAPZ flew briefly at Barton, Bedfordshire. In 1951 it was exhibited at Hendon and at Torbay in 1971 before being rehoused at Old Warden. In 1985 a volunteer restoration team from the Shuttleworth Veteran Aeroplane Society began its complete restoration to flying condition, painting it in its 1930s National Flying Services vivid orange and black scheme. G-AAPZ flew for the first time since 1940 in the hands of Andy Sephton at Old Warden on 26 January 1998.

▲ The National Flying Services logo used on the Desoutter.

▶ Gordon McClymont banks the Desoutter 1 low over Old Warden with the magnificent imposing Jacobean-style mansion (now used mainly as an agricultural college) behind. The estate stretches to nearly six thousand acres and includes most of Old Warden village and many other buildings.

Overleaf: Andy Sephton takes off in G-AAPZ from Old Warden on 26 January 1998: its first flight since 1940.

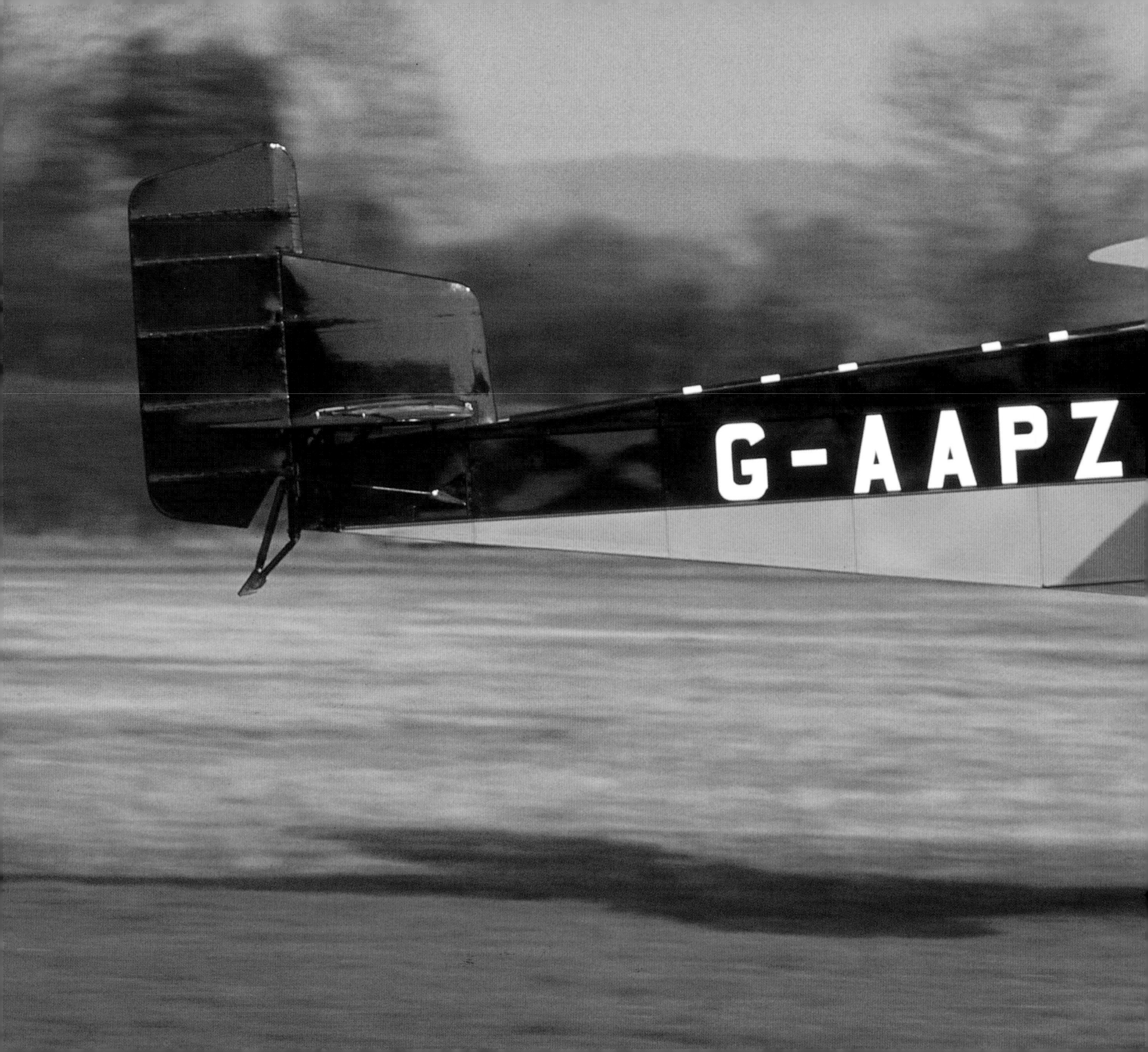
G-AAPZ

1931 de Havilland DH82a Tiger Moth

iger, Tiger. One of the world's most famous training aircraft, the DH82 remained in service with the RAF for fifteen years, from February 1932 until 1947. In Britain, it was not completely replaced in the University Air Squadrons and RAFVR by the Chipmunk until February 1955. In 1960 the Royal Naval Engineering College at Plymouth still possessed eleven airworthy examples for glider towing.

Developed from the Gipsy Moth, the DH82 differed mainly from its predecessor in having staggered and swept-back wings (to enable the front-seat student to evacuate the aircraft more easily in an emergency) and an inverted (Gipsy Major) engine to improve the view forward. The prototype flew for the first time at Stag Lane on 26 October 1931, and the first of the thirty-five Mk I production models, which were powered by 120 hp Gipsy IIIs, were issued to the Central Flying School at Grantham. In 1934 these were followed by an order for fifty Mk II Tigers, which were to be powered by the 130 hp Gipsy Major. This engine now became standard on all the Moths built.

By 1939, more than 1,000 Tigers had been delivered to the RAF Elementary and Reserve Flying Training Schools. In 1941 the Tiger Moths were fitted with anti-spinning strakes on the tail. That same year, after 795 had been built at Hatfield, de Havilland switched over entirely to Mosquito production and Moth manufacturing had to be transferred to the assembly line of Morris Motors Ltd at Cowley, Oxford. By 1945 4,200 Tiger Moths had been built for the RAF and a further 2,949 constructed in Australia, Canada and New Zealand for the Commonwealth Air Training Plan.

T6818/G-ANKT is one of 3,216 DH82as built by Morris Motors Ltd from 1941–45. Its rebuild was carried out almost entirely by two former engineering apprentices at Old Warden. Its first post-restoration flight took place on 3 October 1977.

Trevor Roche at the controls of T6818. ▶

▲ This view of the DH82a Tiger Moth's dual cockpit layout shows to good effect the staggered wing arrangement (achieved by moving all the centre section struts forward of the front cockpit) which enabled the front seat occupant a better chance to egress in an emergency.

◀ The Tiger also differed from the earlier Gipsy Moth in having mainplanes with 19 inches of sweep-back at the tips (to avoid large changes in C of G) and an inverted engine to improve the forward view. Note the yellow square gas-detection panel offset behind the cockpit.

▶ Come in No. 91 your time is up! Tigers are a delight to fly and in World War Two they proved very popular with both instructor and student alike.

1931 Avro Tutor

eacher's pet. In 1932, after three years of comparative trials, the Avro Tutor elementary trainer was declared the winning design to replace the RAF's veteran Avro 504N in Flying Training. The Tutor differed from the 1930 trial batch of twenty-two Avro Trainers in having a 240 hp seven-cylinder Armstrong-Siddeley Lynx IVc in place of the earlier type's five-cylinder Siddeley Mongoose engine. The Tutor also had a cowled engine with a Townend ring around the Lynx, low-pressure tyres and a redesigned fin and rudder. A total of 394 Tutors was built between 1931 and May 1936, the first machines being issued to the Central Flying School. Six Tutors gave a memorable display of aerobatics and inverted flying at the 1933 RAF Hendon Display, and thereafter they became a regular feature of the show. That same year the Tutor replaced the Avro 504N at the RAF College, Cranwell, at No. 5 FTS Sealand, and also replaced the Tiger Moth at No. 3 FTS Grantham. Tutors became the standard equipment at all Flying Training Schools and the University Air Squadrons until 1939.

Today the only survivor is K3215/G-AHSA, which was acquired by the Collection in 1959. One of the main RAF production batch built in 1933, it served with the RAF College, Cranwell, from 1933–36, and then the Central Flying School. Following use as a communications aircraft, it was struck off charge as late as December 1946 and is therefore believed to be the last Tutor in RAF service. G-AHSA passed into private hands at Burnaston, Derby, when Wing Commander Heywood bought the aircraft. It then suffered a crankshaft front end failure during a ground-run in preparation for the film *Reach For The Sky*. A replacement Lynx engine was built by Armstrong-Siddeley at Coventry, using three non-working engines, including one from the College of Aeronautics museum at Cranfield. However, following problems with this engine in 1979 G-AHSA had to be grounded until a replacement Lynx could be found. Despite a world-wide search, no suitable powerplant could be located, so in 1981–82 the troublesome engine was completely rebuilt at Old Warden.

George Ellis putting the Tutor through its paces. ▶

▲ The Tutor is powered by the huge cowled 240 hp seven-cylinder Armstrong-Siddeley Lynx IVc engine.

◀ The Tutor banking over Bedfordshire. In their heyday, Tutors performed memorable displays of aerobatics and inverted flying at RAF Hendon Displays.

▶ Gordon McClymont climbing out at Old Warden.

1932 Arrow Active Mk II

S *lings and Arrows of Outrageous Fortune.* In 1931 the Leeds-based Arrow Company built the first of two Arrow Actives. The company's design team, headed by Arthur Thornton, aimed the Arrow at the advanced flight training and competition market, but production orders never materialised and the company subsequently withdrew from aeroplane construction. G-ABIX, the first of the two Actives, was powered by a 115 hp Cirrus Hermes IIB engine and first flew at Sherburn-in-Elmet. It received a C of A on 21 May 1931. It was later acquired by Alex Henshaw after being unplaced in the 1932 and 1933 King's Cup Air Races. G-ABIX was destroyed on 30 December 1935 when the engine caught fire during high G inverted aerobatics. Henshaw parachuted to safety.

A 120 hp Gipsy III four-cylinder inverted in-line engine was used to power the Active Mk II, which appeared in 1932. G-ABVE was no more successful in the 1932 and 1933 King's Cup Air Races than the first Active and in 1935 it was placed in storage. In 1957 G-ABVE was reconditioned with a 145 hp Gipsy Major IC for use by the Tiger Club. In 1979 the aircraft was acquired by Desmond Penrose and it was raced in the 1980 King's Cup Air Race, finishing second. In 1981 detailed restoration of the aircraft began and G-ABVE reverted to the Gipsy III engine once more. Restoration was completed in April 1989.

This aircraft is privately owned but based with the Shuttleworth Collection

Desmond Penrose aloft in the Active. ▶

◀ ▲ These two views of the Arrow show to great effect the Active's clean lines that should have resulted in it becoming a 1930s racing thoroughbred but surprisingly, given its sporty appearance, the Arrow never quite made the impact in competition flying that its designer, Arthur Thornton, had hoped for.

▶ Desmond Penrose skirts the cloud tops in G-ABVE, a fitting testimony to the superb restoration of the machine which began in 1981 and culminated with the fitting of a Gipsy III engine in April 1989.

1933 HM14 Flying Flea Mk II

allic Gall. French designers were famous (or perhaps infamous) for some weird and wonderful aeroplane and motorcar creations that emerged from the 1930s and 1940s; none more so than Henri Mignet's Pou-de-Ciel, which in those days was better known in Britain as the Flying Flea. Translated literally, Pou-de-Ciel means 'sky louse'! To be fair, the Flea was never designed for plush showrooms, more the back room, or garage, for it was pitched at the do-it-yourself market. Power was provided by a range of motorcycle engines such as the ABC Scorpion, Bristol Cherub, Carden-Ford, Douglas Sprite and Scott.

In 1935 newspapers in England carried stories of a Frenchman and his remarkable home-built aeroplane whose construction was simplicity itself. It could be built for just £140 inclusive of engine, even by those inexperienced with tools. Mignet's highly unconventional creation won many admirers despite misgivings in professional circles. The first British-built specimen, S.V. Appleby's G-ADMH, flew for the first time at Heston on 14 July 1935. Later the Air League even went as far as to encourage the formation of Flea Clubs.

By 1937 'Flea Fever' had broken out in Britain and almost one hundred Pou-de-Ciels had been registered. However, many copies of *Le Sport de l'Air*, the designer's handbook (which sold six thousand copies within a month of going on sale) were probably soon pulped when a series of accidents – four of them fatal – befell the machine. Many of these were caused by control problems. Cautiously, the Air League recommended that the Flea should not be flown until the problems had been rectified. However, full scale wind tunnel tests at Farnborough and in France finally proved conclusively that the Flea was dangerous in the hands of the unwary. (It was found

that in normal flight the Flea was both stable and controllable, but when a downdraught was encountered or the control column was pushed forward a critical incidence was induced which could not be corrected, and this resulted in a nose dive to earth.) A flying ban was imposed by December 1936. Unmoved, Mignet produced a slightly improved version.

HM14 G-AEBB was built by Kenneth William Owen of No. 1 Church Street, Southampton in January–February 1936. It was originally powered by a 1,300 cc Henderson motorcycle engine. It was registered on 24 January 1936 and Owen received an Authorisation to fly from the Air Ministry on 2 March. Despite the flying ban, G-AEBB was granted Authorisation renewals on 4 February 1937 and 1 June 1938. Owen flew G-AEBB at Eastleigh aerodrome before World War Two and then put it into storage. In 1941 he donated the machine to No. 424 (Southampton) Squadron of the ATC. It was used for ground handling and instructional purposes long beyond its usefulness and in May 1967 the squadron gave G-AEBB to the Collection. During restoration by Tony Dowson of the Shuttleworth Volunteer Aeroplane Society (SVAS) the Henderson was replaced by a 25 hp Scott Squirrel engine. G-AEBB was first taxied in public at Old Warden on 8 September 1968. Since its restoration the Flea is technically airworthy, but at Shuttleworth shows no one, wisely, has risked anything other than taxying!

Andy Sephton taxies G-AEBB past the crowd line at Old Warden. Since its restoration, the Flea is capable of flight but in its current configuration, it will never receive a permit to fly. ▶

1934 de Havilland DH87b Hornet Moth

By 1933 de Havilland had realised a need for a Gipsy Moth replacement for the DH80a Puss Moth and the DH85 Leopard Moth for club, instruction and general touring use. Built more for comfort than speed, with an enclosed cabin, cockpit heating and side-by-side seating, the Hornet evolved as a biplane as these wings were less costly to manufacture than those of monoplanes, with their more complicated box spars. The first DH87a was powered by the tried and tested 130 hp Gipsy Major I four-cylinder inverted in-line engine, and flew at Hatfield on 9 May 1934. The first production batch was ready for sale in August 1935.

When it was found that the tapered wings fitted to the first examples led to a tendency, in inexperienced hands, for a wing to drop at low speed, they were later replaced by new, squarer wings. This design was designated the DH87b. Those who had purchased the DH87as were offered trade-in terms to have the mainplanes replaced. The type never achieved the same success as its forebears but the DH87b sold well around the world, and 165 Hornet Moths had been built when production ended in mid-1938.

Only about eight Hornet Moths exist today. G-ADND was completed at Hatfield in 1936 and it was bought by Fairey Aviation in August that year. On 22 February 1940 the aircraft was reserialled W9385 and put to use by No. 3 Coastal Patrol Flight. When it was found that the Hornet Moth was not suitable for coastal patrol, W9385 was passed on to other RAF units until on 1 January 1946 it was released for civilian disposal. G-ADND was acquired by Walter D. Macpherson who used it until July 1953, when former international squash player Peter Quentin Reiss bought the machine. In the 1960s Reiss, a member of the council of the Air Registration Board (ARB), used G-ADND to commute from RAF Andover to Croydon, complete with bowler hat. On retirement Reiss loaned his Hornet to the ARB (now the Airworthiness Division of the CAA) for staff recreational flying from Redhill on condition that it would eventually be presented to the Shuttleworth Collection.

After a groundloop accident at Redhill on 28 March 1971, G-ADND was given that September to Allen Wheeler, trustee of the Shuttleworth Trust. In February 1975 the Hornet was transported to Chester and restoration began. Painted in the Hawker Siddeley Flying Club cream and green colour scheme, it made its first post-restoration flight on 7 May 1976 from Hawarden. After three years at Hawarden G-ADND finally flew to Old Warden on 17 April 1979. The Hornet Moth was officially registered to the Collection in October 1981. In August 1986 the Moth acquired a new paint scheme of mid-blue and white. In June 1994 it reverted to its World War Two camouflage and today flies representing an aircraft of No. 502 Squadron, Coastal Command.

DH87b Hornet Moth over Bedfordshire in the hands of Brian Skillicorn. ▶

1934 de Havilland DH88 Comet

In January 1934 Britain faced the prospect of having no suitable entry for that year's London–Melbourne Centenary Air Race for which Sir MacPherson Robertson had put up a trophy and prizes totalling £15,000 for the winners. With no British Government funding available the de Havilland Company decided to design and build its own long-range racing aeroplane and enter it in the speed section of the race, just ten months away. The company was prepared to share the cost of entry to the race provided enough orders were received. Purchasers were guaranteed a top speed of 200 mph. By the end of February orders for three Comet Racers at a cost of £5,000 each were received. The first order for a Comet Racer was placed by Mr A.O. Edwards, Managing Director of the Grosvenor House Hotel, London, and it would be flown by T. Campbell-Black and C.W.A. Scott. In May Amy (née Johnson) and Jim Mollinson announced their entry in a Comet Racer and the third aircraft was entered by Bernard Rubin, the racing driver, and flown by O. Cathcart Jones and Kenneth Waller.

Building work on three DH88s took place at Stag Lane day and night amid great secrecy before the final assembly and testing at the new factory at Hatfield. The DH88 was a streamlined low-wing monoplane design with a small frontal area, all of which compensated for the low power of its two Gipsy Six engines. The wooden construction and stressed skin covering not only saved weight but also sped up production. Later, similar techniques were successfully applied to the Albatross and Mosquito. However, the radical nature of the Comet caused a few technical problems, not least of which were the complicated French Ratier variable pitch propellers, which it was hoped would give better take-off performance in hot climes. The thin wings meant that the fuel tanks had to be installed in the fuselage and the undercarriage retracted into the lower part of the engine nacelles.

The first DH88 was flown by Captain Hubert Broad on 8 September. On 8 October, the first Comet attained 235 mph at 1,000 ft and 225 mph at 10,000 ft. On 14 October all three Comets, each painted in distinctive racing colours, arrived at Mildenhall, Suffolk. Only 20 of the original 64 entries made the starting line on 20 October. Predictably, Rubin's Comet G-ACSR (Racing No. 19) was in British racing green. The Mollisons' black Comet (G-ACSP) was named *Black Magic*, while *Grosvenor House* (No. 34) was in gleaming red and white and registered G-ACSS. The competitors took off watched by a crowd of 60,000 people. Their route took them by way of five main control points at Baghdad, Allahabad, Singapore, Darwin and Charleville with several intermediate checkpoints in France, Italy, Greece, Asia and Sumatra. The Mollisons arrived at Baghdad first after flying the 2,530 miles non-stop in 12 hours 40 minutes, but they were forced to retire from the race at Allahabad with piston trouble caused by unsuitable fuel.

Scott and Campbell-Black pressed on and completed the 11,300 miles to the Flemington Racecourse in Melbourne with an elapsed time of 70 hours 54 minutes and 18 seconds to win both the speed and handicap race. Scott and Campbell-Black were awarded the £10,000 speed prize and the £650 gold trophy but as each competitor could win just one prize, the handicap prize went to Parmentier and Moll in the DC2. Turner and Pangeborn were third in the Boeing 247D and Jones and Waller's Comet finished fourth (and third in the speed section). On 2 November 1934 Scott and Campbell-Black completed the 23,000-mile return trip with a record time of 13 days 6 hours and 43 minutes. (Tragically, Campbell-Black

was killed at Liverpool Aerodrome in 1936 when his stationary Mew Gull was struck by an incoming Hart.)

Two of the three original Comet Racers were later operated in Europe and Africa but G-ACSS returned to Britain, narrowly avoiding being turned into scrap following a landing accident. Renamed, it went on to take part in further air races. In 1938 it fell into deep neglect but was restored in 1943 and took part in the Festival of Britain in 1951. The aircraft was put on display until 30 October 1965 when it was donated to the Shuttleworth Trust. In 1973 a rebuild was commenced, which would last fourteen years, to restore the Comet to airworthy condition.

In 1984 G-ACSS was transported to Australia to commemorate the 50th Anniversary of the 1934 MacRobertson Air Race. Fully restored to airworthy condition, *Grosvenor House* made its first post-restoration flight on 17 May 1987, in the hands of BAe test pilot George Ellis. Later that month and fifty-three years after leaving the airfield for the memorable flight to Australia, G-ACSS returned to Mildenhall for the US Air Fete. Its first public appearance was at Old Warden for the Shuttleworth Display of 31 May 1987. During repairs following a landing incident,

▲ G-ACSS is one of the most remarkable de Havilland aircraft of all time. Apart from its racing achievements, this streamlined low-wing monoplane design with a small frontal area is credited with having played a significant role in the development of the Mosquito, whose 54 ft 2 in one-piece cantilever wing was built, like the Comet, around a stress-bearing box spar with a thick planking of spruce applied diagonally in two layers.

the castering tailwheel was replaced by a lockable tailwheel (the original tailskid was replaced by a wheel during restoration) and the aircraft flew again on 26 August 1988 at SBAC (Society of British Aircraft Companies) Farnborough.

At Old Warden the longest runway was only half the required length for the Comet to operate safely so the famous old de Havilland airfield at Hatfield, and a hangar generously made available by London Business Aviation, was used to house the Comet in-between flying displays at Old Warden. There, a voluntary team of retired de Havilland employees tended to the Comet's every need. After the closure of Hatfield on 8 April 1993, and with no other suitable airfields available, G-ACSS was moved by road to Old Warden for static display only in May. When completed, the long-awaited extension to Runway 22/04 (from 2,100 ft to 3,900 ft) will mean that the Comet will fly quite happily from Old Warden.

1934 Hawker Hind

fghan Hind. One of the most successful Hart derivatives, the Hind equipped twenty RAF light bomber squadrons during 1935–39. It had an important role as it permitted the formation of many bomber squadrons during the RAF expansion period in preparation for the deliveries of more advanced monoplane bombers. The Hind differed from the Hart in having a fully supercharged 640 hp Rolls-Royce Kestrel V-twelve-cylinder engine, a tailwheel in place of the skid and a cut-away gunner's cockpit similar to that of the Demon. Armament consisted of a Vickers gun firing forward and one Lewis gun firing aft.

The first Hind (K2915) made its maiden flight at Brooklands on 12 September 1934. Production models (which were characterised by rams horn exhaust manifolds) began equipping No. 21 Squadron at Bircham Newton, Norfolk, in December 1935. When production ceased in September 1938 a total of 528 Hinds, including trainers, had been delivered to the RAF. Small numbers of export versions were sold to several foreign air forces, including Afghanistan (which took delivery of eight, followed by twelve ex-RAF models), Persia, Portugal and Switzerland (which ordered one). An ex-seaplane version was later sold to the Yugoslavian Air Force and in 1939–40 Eire purchased six ex-RAF Hinds. The Hind was finally replaced in RAF first-line service in June 1939.

The Collection's Hind, completed in May 1937, is one of the eight machines delivered to the Royal Afghan Air Force in 1938. The last remaining Afghan Hinds were not retired until 1956 and three were acquired for preservation. One went to the RAF Museum in January 1968, one was collected by a Canadian Museum, and one was donated to the Shuttleworth Collection on 21 October 1970 – all having stood at Kabul airfield for many years. The RAF Museum machine was air-freighted to RAF Abingdon but in 1970 the Collection's machine had to be brought back to England overland from Kabul on a hazardous journey of 6,000 miles, using transport provided by the Ford Motor Company. The Hind was then restored at Old Warden and Wing Commander Dicky Martin OBE DFC AFC, the then senior pilot at Old Warden, flew it for the first time in a quarter of a century on 17 August 1981. After a few problems it made its display debut on 25 October, appearing in Afghan markings of silver overall with dark green, black and maroon roundels and rudder stripes. Since 1984 the Hind has worn the markings of No. 15 Squadron RAF (K5414) and from late 1990 has carried four glass-fibre '120 lb GP Mk I bombs' beneath its wings.

◀ No. 15 Squadron flew Hinds at RAF Abingdon from March 1936 until June 1938 and the unit's badge, which appropriately features a Hind, adorns the tail of the aircraft.

▶ Gleam Machine: Gordon McClymont at the controls of the Collection's Hind. Note the four glass-fibre '120 lb GP Mk I bombs', added in late 1990, carried beneath its wings.

▲ K5414, which is powered by a 640 hp Rolls-Royce Kestrel engine, becoming airborne at Old Warden.

Aircraft such as the Hawker Hind, clad in shining metal and colourful liveries, epitomised the almost care-free, golden age of the 1930s RAF biplanes that policed the far-flung territories of the British Empire. Halycon days indeed, repeated now, in the hands of Dodge Bailey in the skies over Bedfordshire.

1935 Percival E2 Mew Gull

The three-seat, single-engine Percival D3 Gull monoplane first appeared in 1932. Percival soon recognised that the D3, and the four-seat Vega Gull, offered potential development of a single-seat racing plane. As a result, six single-seat Type E Mew Gulls were built. They were among the fastest light aeroplanes ever constructed and remained so for more than fifty years.

G-AEXF is the most famous. It was first registered ZS-AHM for Major A.M. Miller and, named *The Golden City/De Goudstad*, was entered in the 1936 Schlesinger Race from Portsmouth to South Africa. Unfortunately, Miller was forced to retire thirty miles from Belgrade with fuel feed problems. In May 1937 this machine, now re-engined with a Gipsy Six Series I and fixed metal airscrew, was bought by Alex Henshaw and reregistered G-AEXF. Henshaw had the machine extensively modified for air racing by Essex Aero engineer, Jack Cross of Comet G-ACSS fame. Henshaw piloted G-AEXF to several racing successes, the most famous being first place in the 1938 King's Cup Air Race with a top speed of 236.25 mph.

Cross carried out further extensive modifications to G-AEXF for an attempt on the 12,754-mile England–Cape Town–England record in February 1939. Fuel capacity was increased from 40 to 87 gallons by inserting a 40-gallon tank directly ahead of the cockpit, while a 7-gallon reserve tank was fitted onto the floor. Henshaw took off in G-AEXF from Gravesend on 5 February

and landed at Cape Town at 7 pm the following day. He took off again a day later and arrived back at Gravesend on 9 February, having completed the 5,997.9-mile trip in 39 hours 36 minutes. The total time for the journey, including 27 hours 19 minutes on the ground at Cape Town, was four days, 10 hours and 20 minutes, giving an average speed of 120 mph. The record-breaking flight is one of aviation's greatest demonstrations of navigational skill and endurance, and stands to this day.

Henshaw sold G-AEXF to Victor Vermorel, a Frenchmen, in July 1940. Vermorel was killed in early 1945 but the Mew Gull miraculously survived the German occupation, and in July 1950 the aeroplane was returned to England by Hugh Scrope. After a crash in 1951 the Gull was rebuilt and Peter Clifford flew G-AEXF to victory in the 1955 King's Cup Air Race. He piloted the aeroplane again in the 1957 race before putting the aeroplane into storage for five years. In October 1962 G-AEXF was purchased by J.E.G. Appleyard and fitted with a Gipsy Queen 2 engine. On 6 August 1965 G-AEXF crashed following engine failure and after many setbacks, was ultimately restored to flying condition. In the spring of 1978 the rebuilt machine flew once more.

In May 1983 an aircraft taxied into G-AEXF while it was parked. It was repaired and flown without incident until 6 May 1985, when the Gull, now owned by Tom Storey, crashed at Redhill. Desmond Penrose, the pilot, survived with only minor injuries. Penrose acquired the Mew from Storey and had it removed to Skysport Engineering, and then to Old Warden, for restoration to its 1939 Cape configuration. G-AEXF made its first post-restoration flight on 19 June 1990.

This aircraft is privately owned but based with the Shuttleworth Collection

◀ G-AEXF, in the hands of Desmond Penrose, becoming airborne at Old Warden.

1935 BA Swallow

S *wallows and Amazons.* In the late 1920s some examples of the German-designed Klemm L25 two-seat, low-wing monoplane were imported into Britain by Major E.F. Stephen. By 1933 he had sold seventeen L25s and that same year he established the British Klemm Aeroplane Company to build these machines under licence at Hanworth. The first six machines retained the 75 hp Salmson engine which had powered the Klemms since production began in 1927, but thereafter the 90 hp Pobjoy Cateract III seven-cylinder uncowled radial was used. By 1935 the British-built L25 had undergone a major redesign, with squared-off wingtips, rudder, tailplane and fuselage top-decking being carried out to permit quantity production. The new design was designated the Swallow 2 and a new company, the British Manufacturing Co., was set up to sell them.

The forty-second airframe built in Britain was powered by the 90 hp Blackburn Cirrus Minor four-cylinder, in-line engine and subsequent models were powered by this and the Cateract engine. Of the 105 Swallows built at Hanworth, 98 were acquired by flying clubs or private buyers. One of the major users was Blackburn Aircraft Co, which operated 15 Cirrus-powered models at No. 4 Elementary and Reserve Flying School at Brough in East Yorkshire.

G-AFCL, which was loaned to the Collection in 1978, was built in November 1937 and registered to W.L. Hope. Immediately after World War Two it was owned by G.H. Forsaith, who based it at Thruxton. In May 1965 it passed to Bert Etheridge, a wood craftsman at Old Warden. G-AFCL was restored for the Collection by Tony Dowson, a member of the Shuttleworth Veteran Aeroplane Society.

One swallow does not make a summer so they say, but G-AFCL, in its striking canary yellow livery, is always a welcome arrival overhead at Old Warden. ▶

This aircraft is privately owned but based with the Shuttleworth Collection

1935 Gloster Gladiator

This remarkable, sturdy biplane fighter was powered by an 840 hp Bristol Mercury IX and armed with two .303-inch Browning machine-guns in the fuselage, plus one under each wing. By the time production ceased in April 1940, 480 had been delivered to the RAF, 60 Sea Gladiators to the FAA and 216 Gladiators to 12 other countries.

The Gladiator first entered RAF service with No. 72 Squadron in February 1937 and with No. 3 Squadron the following month. In May 1940 Gladiators of Nos 607 and 615 Squadrons of the AASF (Advanced Air Striking Force) fought in Belgium and France, and later defended the fleet at Scapa Flow. In April and May 1940 No. 263 Squadron's outnumbered Gladiators fought valiantly against the *Luftwaffe* in Norway. Operating from HMS *Glorious* in May with Sea Gladiators of No. 804 Squadron FAA, the Gladiators destroyed thirty-six enemy aircraft for the loss of only two in combat. No. 263 Squadron flew its last patrol on 7 June. On 8 June HMS *Glorious* was sunk by the battle-cruisers *Scharnhorst* and *Gneisenau* and all the Gladiator pilots were lost.

From 11–28 June 1940 six Gladiators flown by RAF pilots constituted the entire air defence of Malta. The first Italian air raid on the island took place on the morning of 11 June and the unescorted force of bombers was broken up by two of the Gladiators. Contrary to the legend of 'Faith, Hope and Charity', only

three air raids took place between 11–30 June and it is almost certain the 'six' Gladiators were so named for morale boosting purposes.

In August 1940 Gladiators equipped No. 247 Squadron at Roborough, and were responsible for the defence of Plymouth Docks during the Battle of Britain. The Gladiator's greatest successes were against the *Regia Aeronautica* in Greece. By the end of 1940, Flight Lieutenant M.T. St J. Pattle DFC is known to have shot down at least twenty-four enemy aircraft in a Gladiator while flying from bases in Greece. The Gladiator continued its first-line service with the RAF until 1941 and was also used in other roles until 1945, notably on meteorological flights.

For many years the Collection's Gladiator (G-AMRK), which was manufactured in 1938, appeared as L8032 with blue and red fuselage bars to represent an aircraft of No. 72 Squadron. L8032 was almost lost in 1942, when Jack Towey, who flew the aircraft on thirty-four sorties from Detling in World War Two, had an 'engine cut' at 12,000 ft above one of the forts in the Thames estuary and decided to bale out. Towey actually climbed onto the port wing, then changed his mind because of a heavy sea mist. Struggling back into the cockpit, he headed for Detling, twelve miles away, where, trimmed to glide at 45–50 knots, the Gladiator completed a circuit before touching down safely!

Early in 1948 L8032, the last Gladiator I, and N5903, a Gladiator II,

▲ For many years the Collection's Gladiator appeared in the dark earth and green camouflage scheme representing N2308 HP-B of No. 247 Squadron, based at Roborough in 1940.

▲ The Collection's Gladiator now appears in the silver and red colours of the Norwegian Army Air Force and here it is being flown by Andy Sephton.

arrived at Hucclecote. In 1950 they were transferred to the Air Service Training schools at Hamble and Ansty respectively, for employment as ground instruction airframes. Vivian Bellamy, an ex-FAA Gladiator pilot, of Flightways at Eastleigh, bought them both for a 'peppercorn' sum and relocated them to Thruxton, Wiltshire. He removed the Mercury XI from L8032 and re-engined it with the Mercury VIII from N5903 but retained the XI's reduction gear and the two-bladed wooden propeller. In spring 1952, with the civil registration G-AMRK, Bellamy flew it for the first time. In August 1953, when he could no longer afford to fly G-AMRK, Gloster bought it back for £200. Gloster test pilots Dicky Martin and Geoff Worrall flew it in air displays until 1956 when Gloster decided to restore the

aeroplane. Refurbished by Gloster apprentices, an authentic gunsight and armament was installed. Then in spring 1958, with Air Ministry permission, it was given No. 72 Squadron 'B' Flight markings and the spurious serial K8032 (which had been worn by an earlier Gladiator flown by that squadron).

With the closure of Gloster, on 17 November 1960 Hawker Siddeley presented the Gladiator to the Shuttleworth Collection. From 1990 the 'Glad' was displayed in a green and brown camouflage and black and white underside scheme to represent N2308 HP-B of No. 247 Squadron at Roborough in 1940. The Gladiator now appears in *Haerens Flyvapen* (Norwegian Army Air Force) markings. (Late in 1937 Norway bought six Gladiator Mk Is from Gloster and six Mk IIs in 1939.)

Gordon McClymont roars low over Old Warden to set the pulses racing. ▲

With its 840 hp Bristol Mercury engine running, the 'Glad' prepares to taxi out at Old Warden. ◄

1937 Miles Magister

The 'Maggie' was the first monoplane trainer to be issued to RAF elementary flying training, the first (L5913) being delivered to the Central Flying School in September 1937. It was of all-wood construction and powered by a 130 hp Gipsy Major I four-cylinder, inverted in-line engine. By 1941 some 1,293 examples had been built by Miles Aircraft Ltd at Woodley, Reading. The Magister equipped no fewer than sixteen Elementary Flying Training Schools throughout World War Two. Post-war, not unsurprisingly, many hundreds of surplus Magisters found their way onto the civil market, yet only three are in flying condition today. The Shuttleworth machine never held a civil registration, although when it first arrived at Old Warden it was thought to be P6382. However, inspection of the aircraft's log-book revealed an earlier change of fuselage!

Andy Sephton at the controls of the Maggie near Old Warden. ▶

◀ ▲ Andy Sephton piloting P6382 over the lake behind the mansion at Old Warden. When one considers that P6382's wooden construction dates back to the 1930s, it is not too surprising that it is one of only three preserved airworthy Magisters worldwide. The Collection's Magister is powered by a 130 hp DH Gipsy Major I four-cylinder inverted in-line engine.

▶ Andy Sephton aloft in P6382. The white square offset behind the cockpit is representative of the gas detection panel used on aircraft in World War Two.

1941 Hawker Sea Hurricane IB

The Hurricane is the most famous in the long line of Hawker single-seat fighters. In the Battle of Britain it was flown by about six in every ten squadrons and accounted for more enemy aircraft destroyed than any other type of British aircraft. Although Sydney (later Sir Sydney) Camm's immortal design was fabric-covered, its construction was tubular steel and proved easier to build than the Spitfire, which used a metal stressed-skin monocoque structure with only the control surfaces being fabric-covered. Like the Spitfire, the Hurricane was powered by the Rolls-Royce Merlin and was armed with eight .303-inch Browning machine-guns in the wings.

The Hurricane made its maiden flight on 6 November 1935 and the aircraft's less complicated construction (compared to the Spitfire) permitted quantity production to begin immediately. (In 1939 metal-covered wings began to be fitted on the production lines instead of fabric-covered wings.) By 7 August 1940 2,309 Hurricanes had been delivered, compared with 1,383 Spitfires.

By early August 1940 Hurricane Is equipped thirty-two squadrons of the RAF (the Spitfire equipped eighteen and a half squadrons). Four Hurricane squadrons were despatched to France at the outbreak of war as part of the Advanced Air Striking Force and the Air Component. In the first twelve months of the war, up until the end of the Battle of Britain, the Hurricane shot down more than 1,500 enemy aircraft.

The Sea Hurricane is often the forgotten relation, yet it was used aboard merchant ships, where it was catapulted into action, and aboard escort-carriers. The Sea Hurricane IA began equipping the Fleet Air Arm when No. 880 Squadron was issued with the type in January 1941 for embarkation onboard HMS *Furious* in July. It thus became the first British single-seat monoplane fighter to go to sea aboard carriers of the Royal Navy. A Sea Hurricane first destroyed an enemy aircraft on 21 July when a Dornier Do 18 was shot down off Norway. Sea Hurricanes carried out valuable fighter defence of convoys onboard the escort-carriers heading to Russia, while in the Mediterranean they carried out equally important duties flying combat patrols from larger aircraft carriers for convoys heading for Malta.

Sea Hurricanes were progressively armed with 20 mm cannon in place of machine-guns and they held the line at sea until Allied naval aircraft entered service. By the end of 1943 the Sea Hurricane had largely disappeared from first-line service, and had been replaced by Seafires and Hellcats on the large carriers and by Wildcats on the escort-carriers.

Hurricane IB Z7015 was built as a Mk I by the Canadian Car and Foundry Company at the Kingston Ontario plant in the winter of 1940–41. It was crated and

With the cockpit canopy drawn back, Andy Sephton pilots the Collection's
Sea Hurricane high above Bedfordshire on a sunny summer's day. ▶

shipped to England and was taken on charge at RAF Henlow on 18 March 1941. On 27 June it was converted by General Aircraft Ltd to a Sea Hurricane IB. On 29 July 1941 Z7015 was issued to No. 880 Squadron, which became the first FAA squadron to be equipped with Hurricanes on 15 March 1941. By 14 October 1941 No. 880 Squadron had embarked on HMS *Indomitable*, but Z7015 did not go with them. It remained in the UK and in 1942–43 served with No. 759 Squadron. At the end of 1943 Z7015 was delivered to Loughborough College and used as a ground instructional airframe for eighteen years. In 1961 Z7015 and Spitfire Vc AR501 were exchanged by the College for a Jet Provost TI in the Shuttleworth Collection. Z7015 was used as a taxying aircraft in the film *The Battle of Britain*, after which it was partially restored at Staverton before moving to Duxford where it was restored jointly by SVAS (Shuttleworth Veteran Aeroplane Society) volunteers and the Imperial War Museum. At Duxford on 16 September 1995, piloted by Andy Sephton, Z7015 flew for the first time since its rebuild. This Hurricane and its Merlin III engine are the earliest airworthy examples anywhere.

◀ ▲ These two unusual but nevertheless welcome views of the Sea Hurricane, with its stubby exhausts and dependable Merlin, confirm all that was best in British design and Canadian co-production which contributed so much to final victory in World War Two.

1941 Supermarine Spitfire Vc

The Spitfire first flew on 5 March 1936 and is the most famous aircraft ever to see service with the RAF. It was the only British fighter to remain in continuous production throughout World War Two. In all, 27 different marks saw service up until 1947 and total Spitfire/Seafire production reached 22,759. Numerically, the Mk V was the most important Spitfire produced, with a total of 6,464 (94 Mk Vas, 3,923 Mk Vbs, and 2,447 Mk Vcs) built.

Intended initially as a stop-gap, the Mk V was basically a Mk I or II structurally strengthened to accommodate the heavier and more powerful Rolls-Royce 1,440 hp Merlin 45 series V-12 engine in place of the 1,175 hp Merlin XII. Another important difference between the Mk II and the Mk V was the introduction of metal ailerons, compared with the former's fabric type. The rate of roll at high speeds was doubled. The Mk Va still carried eight .303-inch Browning machine-guns but the Mk Vb housed two 20 mm cannon and four machine-guns. The Mk Vc introduced a 'universal' wing capable of housing eight machine-guns, or two cannon and four machine-guns, or four cannon. A drop tank or 500 lb bomb could be carried under the centre fuselage. The Spitfire Va entered service with No. 92 Squadron at Biggin Hill in February 1941 and, ultimately, it equipped no fewer than seventy-one UK-based RAF squadrons.

Spitfire Vs equipped Nos 71, 121 and 133 'Eagle' Squadrons, which were later absorbed into the 4th Fighter Group, 8th Air Force, at Debden. The Debden 'Eagles' retained their Mk Vbs until conversion to the P-47C Thunderbolt in March 1943. Other US units equipped with the Mk V included the 31st and 52nd Fighter Groups, the 67th Observation Group at Membury, Wiltshire, and the 7th Photo Reconnaissance Group was also equipped with a few Mk Vs.

About 180 Spitfire Mk Is and Mk IIs In RAF service were converted to Mk V standard and took part in daylight *Rhubarb* low-level sweeps over enemy-occupied Europe during 1941–42. By late August 1942 three RAF squadrons were equipped with the tropicalised Spitfire Mk V in North Africa. Some 247 Mk Vcs were delivered to Australia in August 1942 and the type went on to improve its combat record against the Japanese. In October 1943 Spitfire Vs began operations in Burma. Altogether, four squadrons in the Far East were equipped with Spitfire Vs.

AR501 is still the only Spitfire flying in the world with an original three-bladed metal propeller, which was originally fitted to the Sea Hurricane. ▲

▲ Ex-Empire Test Pilots School and currently Virgin
Atlantic Captain Dave Mackay, aloft in AR501.

In Europe the Spitfire V's ascendancy over the *Luftwaffe* largely continued until late 1941 when the Focke Wulf 190A completely out-classed the Mk V, except that the Spitfire had a much better turning circle. Mk Vs had their wings clipped in an attempt to reduce the gap in performance. Trials carried out by the Air Fighting Development Unit at Duxford late in 1942 showed that the removal of the Mk V's metal wingtips considerably improved the type's rate of roll. It also improved acceleration, speed and dive characteristics below 10,000 ft. A further improvement in low altitude performance was gained when the Mk V was fitted with a Merlin 50M engine. This was similar to the Merlin 45 but had a 'cropped' supercharger impeller as well as a diaphragm carburettor. (In December 1941 the Mk V had become the first of the Spitfires to use a successful diaphragm carburettor to prevent engine cut out during manoeuvres which imposed negative-G on the aircraft.) The low altitude-rated Merlin and clipped wing combination was designated Spitfire LF V.

LF Vc AR501/G-AWII, owned and operated by the Collection, is a Westland Aircraft machine built at Yeovil, Somerset, which rolled off the production line on 29 June 1942. On 19 July it was issued to No. 310 (Czech) Squadron (motto: We Fight To Rebuild) at Exeter in Devon. AR501 was coded NN-A and made its first operational sortie on 3 August when Sergeant Skach flew a 1 hour 25 minutes evening patrol over a convoy in the Channel two miles off Start Point. NN-A operated with No. 310 Squadron until late in 1943 when it passed to another Czech Squadron, No. 312. AR501 was used later by the RAF Central Gunnery School, and post-war it served as an instructional airframe at Loughborough College. After its transfer to the Collection in 1961, AR501 was restored to flying condition for the film *The Battle of Britain* and then stored for several years at Old Warden. A later restoration was carried out by a volunteer team at Duxford.

This view shows to great effect the clipped
wings that characterised the Mk Vc. ▶

1942 Westland Lysander IIIA

Known as the 'Lizzie', the Lysander is undoubtedly one of the most famous aircraft to serve the RAF. It is perhaps best remembered for infiltrating and retrieving SOE (Special Operations Executive) and OSS (Office of Strategic Services) agents, or 'Joes', from under the noses of the enemy in occupied countries in World War Two.

The prototype first flew on 15 June 1936 and production models entered service in June 1938, mainly as artillery spotting and reconnaissance aircraft. Although armed with just two fixed .303 in machine-guns in the wheel spats and a single .303 in the rear cockpit, in November 1939 a Lysander shot down a Heinkel He 111. It was the first enemy bomber to fall in BEF (British Expeditionary Force) territory. The Lysander could also carry eight light bombs beneath its undercarriage spat winglets. The Lizzie also carried out many attacks on German positions during the Dunkirk evacuation and continually dropped badly needed supplies to the beleaguered BEF.

In all, 1,428 Lysanders had been built in Britain when production ceased in January 1942. They were operated in the Western Desert, Palestine and India, and when superseded by Tomahawks in Army Co-operation squadrons they began a new career in ASR (Air Sea Rescue) and were also used as target-tugs.

Able to operate from improvised landing strips and using its short-field capability to best advantage, the Lysander III (SD or 'Special Duty') was fitted with a 150-gallon long-range tank and a side ladder. It was operated with Nos 138, 148 and 161 Squadrons and No. 357 Squadron in the Far East.

V9441/G-AZWT is a Lysander IIIA (347 were built) completed in Canada and it is powered by a 870 hp Bristol Mercury XX nine-cylinder radial. V9441

served as a target-tug with the RCAF until acquired by farmer and wartime pilot Wes Agnew of Manitoba, who bought the aircraft from Canadian Crown Assets. In 1971 V9441 was acquired by Sir William Roberts, founder of the Strathallan Collection, and put on temporary display. Restoration to flying condition began in 1978 and in August 1979 engine runs commenced. The first post-restoration flight took place on 14 December 1979, but the aircraft logged only twenty-eight hours before being relegated to static display. The Shuttleworth Collection acquired V9441 early in 1998. The aircraft is painted in the colours of No. 309 (Polish) Squadron, an Army Co-operation unit, and in the winter of 1999/2000 received a 150-gallon long-range dummy petrol tank and ladder, to complete authentification. V9441 is now the only flyable Lysander in the UK.

Immortalised as the 'Lizzie', the Collection's Lysander is now the only flyable example in the UK. ▲

▲ Lysander III bedecked in No. 309 (Polish) Squadron colours. In 1940
Flt Lt Konrad 'Wiewiorka' (Squirrel) Stembrowicz, a recently arrived Polish
fighter pilot in Britain, 'went looking for Messerschmitts over London' in a
Lysander armed only with a few rounds of ammunition!

▲ Chris Morris, Chief Engineer, watches attentively as George Ellis fires up the 870 hp Bristol Mercury XX. George began his flying career with the Cambridge University Air Squadron before joining the RAF in 1968 and flying Lightnings in Germany. In 1980 he joined BAe as a test pilot and later became the Deputy Senior Pilot at the Shuttleworth Collection.

▶ Dodge Bailey draws in close. As far as Allied agents were concerned there was no greater sight for sore eyes than the welcome appearance of the Lysander as it touched down in moonlit fields in France and the Low Countries to snatch them to safety under the very noses of the enemy.

Flying the Collection Andy Sephton

There is a popular misconception that suggests the Collection's aircraft are difficult to fly. Fortunately this is not the case, for if it were difficult to fly them they would not have been so successful in their day. In Edwardian times aviation pioneers not only built their own machines, they tested them and learned to fly them without instruction. Certainly they had their accidents (who wouldn't under similar circumstances) but in time success arrived.

The same argument holds true when we look at later machines. Would the SE5a of World War I or the Spitfires and Hurricanes of World War II have been so successful in the hands of the average youth had they been difficult to fly? It has to be said, however, that a pilot with experience of only modern machines, be it at the private, commercial or military level, would find flight in a Collection aircraft something of a challenge.

So how do we solve this paradox? Perhaps a better description of the Collection's aircraft would be that they are different rather than difficult.

To some degree most of the machines, when compared to their modern counterparts, are unstable about at least one of their axes. The Tiger Moth, for example, wanders in yaw (direction) and requires active feet on the part of the pilot to maintain directional control. In a similar way, the Hurricane is lively in pitch.

If we go to the early models of the Collection and look at the Blériot, we find a machine that suffers from roll reversal, i.e. when we move the control column to the right the machine rolls left. The aerodynamic explanation is outside the scope of this book, but suffice to say that the characteristic is normal and requires that the machine be steered by rudder rather than by roll.

A similar story can be found if one looks at the operation of the engines. Modern engines with modern control systems allow carefree handling of the throttle. This includes slam accelerations and decelerations, which are taught as a fundamental characteristic of piston engines during basic pilot training. If this is tried on the Mercury engine in the Gladiator or Lysander then the pilot would be rewarded with an immediate rich cut that would take at least 30 seconds to clear. On most of the older engines, and new ones for that matter, rapid throttle demand can also lead to excessive engine wear from shock loading. In the Pobjoy, it could result in engine failure due to a sheared magneto drive shaft.

As we go back in time to earlier engines, we find that the pilot has to control the oil feed manually, as on the ABC engine in the Wren and the Anzani in the Blériot. On the rotaries, he has to do the same with the fuel. The rotary can be modulated by judicious use of the control levers from about 800 rpm to 1,200 rpm to produce between 50% and 100% thrust. To reduce power for taxi or descent, the engine is switched off by cutting the ignition or by turning off the fuel. The fuel lever settings are, however, critical and the pilot must be in constant touch with his engine to keep it running. A petrol lever wrongly positioned by only a millimetre or so could lead to a rich cut that would take up to 30 seconds to clear in flight.

The Shuttleworth philosophy is to demonstrate the sight and sound of the machines in the air. For safe flight then, it is necessary for the pilots to relearn the skills of yesteryear. We achieve this by carefully unteaching modern techniques and reteaching the piloting skills necessary for each older machine. For example, as a pilot progressed through the Collection, one route might be to pass from the relatively benign handling characteristics of the Moths through the reduced control power of the Elf to the limited control of the LVG. From here he may learn the skill necessary to control the wing warping of the Avro Triplane and then to the further limited control of the Blériot or Deperdussin. Each stage in the process would take him further away from today's control skills towards the more demanding characteristics of the earlier aircraft. The process takes time. The piloting skills required at each level must be mastered

before progressing, or regressing, to the next. With the knowledge gained *en route*, coupled with a sound understanding of the aerodynamic and mechanical characteristics of the earlier machines, we find it is possible to demonstrate the Collection's aircraft with confidence and safety.

So, are they difficult to fly? Not at all. Challenging, yes; different, yes, but certainly not difficult.

◄ Andy Sephton, the Collection's Senior Pilot, in the cockpit of the Gladiator. Andy won an ATC flying scholarship to gain his PPL in 1967. After joining the RAF he flew many types at squadron level before becoming an instructor and test pilot. He is currently chief test pilot at Rolls-Royce.

▲ Andy Sephton is all smiles in the cockpit of the English Electric Wren.

Engineering the Collection Chris Morris

Many times we have to correct the person, or article, by patiently explaining that all the artefacts at Old Warden Aerodrome are, or will be, in full working order, whether it be a bicycle, horse-drawn carriage, motorbike, car or aircraft, just as originally designed. This is the Shuttleworth Collection where all the aircraft are maintained in flying condition, through a system of maintenance, inspection and certification, governed by a statutory document called the Air Navigation Order, and managed by the Civil Aviation Authority (CAA). Engineers, granted licences by the CAA, authorise the maintenance and inspection work carried out on the aircraft, and ultimately sign the documents allowing the aircraft to fly.

The Collection is an educational charity, which means that the aircraft must remain as original as possible – all rebuilds and maintenance work will try to retain the designers' intentions, whether it be materials, design or finish. The Collection is housed in seven aircraft hangars and open to the paying public for 360 days of the year, so the hangars and their contents have to be serviceable and presentable.

As may be seen from the aforementioned, severe conflicting requirements have to be balanced to achieve our aims. Another oft asked question difficult to answer is 'Where do you get your spares from ?' This is where the expertise and experience of the engineering section takes each decision on its own, and balances firstly safety, secondly originality and then the cost and time-scale. Some of the very early aircraft probably had bamboo primary or secondary structures, covered with cotton sealed with flour size. We have had to move on a little from there, but almost all of the other materials used from the beginning of World War One are still available, i.e. steel tube, Irish linen, ash, spruce, birch ply and cordage, albeit now of higher and more consistent quality. The glues, dopes, paints and celluloids are much improved, but carry out the same task as the originals.

Spares often cause us problems, but never beat us. We have an excellent rapport with museums and private collections around the world, and good contacts with small businesses. Components can often be exchanged outright, or borrowed. The odd component we put into our stores can often be brought out and reclaimed by modern methods by electro plating, rebuilding and remachining, or used as a pattern to cast a new item. Modern CAD-CAM machinery and suitable materials will often produce a component identical to the original. There are still manufacturers that can produce small quantities of piston rings, leather cup

Chris Morris, Chief Engineer, joined the Collection in 1979 after many years with the de Havilland Aircraft Co. at Hatfield. ▲

washers, copper asbestos gaskets. They can manually manipulate and weld complex aluminium panels, produce radiators, overhaul 95-year-old magnetos, fully overhaul the de Havilland and Dowty Rotol propellers and supply parts for Merlin engines etc. If these sources fail, there is always someone who can produce the required component. Supply and Demand works well.

Any major maintenance required usually starts just after the last open day of the year in October, with inhibiting the engines internally with a wax compound, removing batteries and stacking Hangar 1 (the heated maintenance hangar) for the first aircraft requiring attention. Any minor snags or adjustments during the season are rectified there and then; it is rare for an aircraft to miss a flying display. All the planned tasks start then, such as propeller, undercarriage, engine, radiator or wing removal. Modifications or additions start at this stage too, similar to the manufacture and attachment of a dummy long-range tank and side ladder for the Lysander. With over 30 aircraft requiring an annual Permit to Fly (aircraft MOT) nearly half are renewed during the winter months before the first open day in May, leaving two to three per month during the season.

Rebuilds, such as the Desoutter and Martlet are continued on an as-and-when basis during the year, the aim being to complete one project before starting another. Other major planned tasks are engine rebuilds and fabric recover, but these are fortunately few and far between.

As in all walks of life, rules and regulations are becoming more complex; paperwork proliferates and the culture of blame leading to the very real threat of legal action if something does go seriously wrong, has to be borne in mind in all our decision making. Our duty of care to the public, to our pilots and staff and to everyone involved in the operation of the Collection is a major preoccupation.

The expertise of the Collection is therefore not only directed at the difficult enough task of actually flying some of the earliest and historically valuable aeroplanes in the world, but doing so in the full glare of modern safety requirements. That this challenge is met with a range of types from veteran machines of primitive design to 50-year-old fighting aircraft of World War Two is no mean achievement by the men on the hangar floor. Long may we be able to continue to exercise our skills and pass them on to those who will come after.

Photographic credits

Colour Photography © John M. Dibbs/The Plane Picture Company

The following photographers also kindly contributed images:

© Ian Frimston/Fuji Lab

p17, p18, p20 (top), p22, p26 (bottom), p28, p40 (top), p60, p87 and p98.

© David Macready
p20 (bottom), p21, p49, p63 and p82.

© Martin W. Bowman
p45, p83, p100 and p101.